A SUMMER FOR A LIFETIME

The Life and Times of George I. Purdy

by George I. Purdy
as told to Thomas Caldwell

Foreword by Michael J. Mansfield

LOST
COAST
PRESS
Fort Bragg
California

Lost Coast Press
155 Cypress Street
Fort Bragg, CA 95437
phone: (800) 773-7782 fax: (707) 964-7531

Publisher's Cataloging-in-Publication
(*Provided by Quality Books, Inc.*)

Purdy, George I.
    A summer for a lifetime : the life and times of
George I Purdy / as told to Thomas Caldwell. --
1st ed.
    p. cm.
    LCCN: 99-75429
    ISBN: 1-882897-45-5

    1. Purdy, George I. 2. World War, 1939-1945--
Personal narratives, American. 3. World War,
1939-1945--Campaigns--Japan. 4. World War,
1939-1945--Japan. I. Caldwell, Thomas, 1962-
II. Title.

D767.2.P87 2000   940.54'25
                                   QBI99-1450

Manufactured in Canada

Acknowledgments

WHEN I WAS ASKED TO LIST THE PEOPLE that I wanted to thank for their help, friendship and support over the years, I thought it would be a rather easy task. I was wrong. There are so many years, so many names, and so little space. I will do my best:

It is impossible to succeed in life without great friends with whom to work and play. Thanks to Fred Harris, a successful businessman and a close friend for thirty-five years; Joe Diele, a fellow 33rd degree Scottish-Rite Mason with whom I have had the honor of sharing many Masonic endeavors; Phil Campanella, the "Mr. Do Good" of Japan's Kansai region; Dr. Allen L. Robinson, who headed the committee that made this book a reality; Jim Adachi, my successor as president of the American Chamber of Commerce in Japan; Bill Kyle; Bill Dizer, my favorite expert on handling small boats; Henry Yaskal; Kaoru Ogimi, a world-class yachtsman; and Ed Beeby, a fellow boating enthusiast .

Among the people that I hold in very high regard are former Senator and U.S. Ambassador to Japan Mike Mansfield, whose eleven years in Japan were some of the most productive for U.S.-Japan relations; retired Admirals Suteo Ishida and Ryohei Ohga, who both served as Chiefs of Staff of the Japanese Maritime Self-Defense Forces; Koichiro Hattori; Ralph Kestenbaum; business associates Ryuko Hira, Kris Panjabi and Charlotte Kennedy-Takahashi; publisher Corky Alexander; submariner Jim Murphy; former U.S. Navy Captain Tom Hennesy; Bill Bademan; Marvin Bledso; Rex Sebastion; Kunihiko Tanda; and Toichiro Hirano, one of my first Japanese friends and business associates.

Special thanks to former ACCJ presidents Tom Jordan and Bill

Beagles, who have made the later years of my career as interesting and exciting as the first. There is also Bob Licciardi, who bought my beloved boat and became a great friend in the process; my friend and health consultant, John Wocher; Al Jenks and son; former U.S. Naval Attache in Tokyo, Scotty Van Hoften; Charlie Swift; and Yuichi Yamamoto, who took control of my business and continues to do a terrific job in running it.

Of all the friends and adopted brothers I could have had, nobody could have played the part better than Harry Holloway. Our eighty-year, close friendship must have set a record. There is also my family living in the United States, especially my two grandchildren, John and Hunter Purdy, their children and their mother, Dobree, whose long-distance love and devotion have meant so much to me.

There is not enough room to formally thank the spouses of all the people I have mentioned, but I would like to do so. I especially want to thank the very special spouse with whom I have spent some of the happiest and most rewarding years of my life: my wife, partner and best friend, Midori. Her affection and love have been indispensable to me and the life that you will learn about in this book.

To everyone who has been there for me and with me through the years: *domo arigato gozaimashita.*

> George I. Purdy
> Zushi Marina, Kanagawa
> June 1998

Foreword

by Michael J. Mansfield
United States Ambassador to Japan (1977–88)
United States Senator from Montana (1952–77)

A Summer for a Lifetime is the story of George Purdy's outstanding career, his devotion to duty, and the friendship he showed towards the people with whom he came in contact. His life, based on understanding, experience and humor, is a compilation of his many accomplishments. It is, in effect, a history of the times through which he and his wife Midori have lived.

George Purdy's knowledge of the facts, combined with his application of them to the realities of his times, is superb. He not only helped make history, but he lived it as well. His wit, wisdom and statesmanship represented our country at its best. If you want to increase your knowledge of the past, as well as your knowledge of the present, then this is the book to read. It is a well-balanced American canvas based on firsthand knowledge, extensive experience and deep understanding.

Michael J. Mansfield
The Mansfield Center for Pacific Affairs
Washington, D.C., August 28, 1998

Author's Introduction

Zushi Marina is a strange-sounding place to those who do not live in Japan. For want of a better description, it is Japan's Marina Del Rey. Only the most ambitious and successful can afford to live there, while the ordinary Japanese citizen can only visit.

As the pleasure craft return from sea against a sunset found only in the Far East, an elderly man stands on the pier next to another, younger fellow. Neither are natives of Japan, but for the rest of their days, no matter where the winds of life lead them, they will never be able to completely sever their links to the land that has become their adoptive home.

They stand and talk of things that would have passed as small talk, if the sun did not so brilliantly illuminate the late afternoon sky. The rays of light add more emphasis to their words than any tone of voice or exclamation mark ever could.

A fair-sized cabin cruiser slowly pulls up to the pier. The older man jumps into action like a dockhand in his twenties. He calls out to the pleasure craft, asking them to throw him a line. With the skill of a lifelong sailor, he catches the rope and ties it quickly and securely to the dock.

A short conversation ensues between the older man and the crew of the pleasure craft. He compliments them on the fish they caught. A wide smile lights up his face as he speaks to them in his friendly, yet fragmented, Japanese. The sun sinks deeper into the blue Pacific. Another day has come to an end.

The younger man looks on, scribbling notes, and taking in the moment. He knows that memories are the best way to remember such times. The best photographs are never taken, and the greatest quotes are never recorded. Still, he tries to document the moment.

From the time that I first met George Purdy in 1986, I knew that he was something special; not because he lived through one of the most extraordinary periods in human history, but because, through it all, he maintained his humanity, self-respect and dignity—something few people who reach his level of success and social position are able to do.

What began more than a decade ago as a series of interviews is now the book you find before you. It is the chronology of his life, as well as a written record of the man's unique philosophy and insight into human existence.

Nobody writes a book without a great deal of help from others. Many people think that writing a book is not a difficult task. Depending on the type of book that one writes, it can best be described as having a weight tied around your neck while trying to swim a race; it never leaves you. You must endure it until you reach the end.

As for subject matter, only one thing is worse than writing a book: writing a biography—especially if the person is still alive. With every meeting, there is always another story, another insight, or another side that makes completion of the work as difficult as a task laid upon the classical heroes by the gods of ancient times. Still, it has its moments. In the end, it was worth the time and effort.

With that said, I would like to thank those who helped me with my side of the task: the members of The Phoenix Project for their support, enthusiasm and, especially, patience; to Dr. Allen Robinson whose encouragement and friendly prodding were a Godsend.

Special thanks to Bill Clough at UPI Radio, a literary wordsmith if ever there was one; Yoichi Clark Shimatsu, a brilliant editor, mentor and teacher, for all of the encouragement, analysis and coffee; Midori Purdy, George's better half who, besides being a gracious hostess, is probably one of the most organized people in postwar Japanese history.

Yet, the real thanks go to George I. Purdy, who has lived, and is continuing to live, a fascinating life. It is a true honor to be given the task of recording his life for future generations.

One final thought before you begin reading: although George Purdy is a most interesting fellow, I am filled with a touch of sadness knowing that all the other "George Purdys" of the world live their lives unnoticed by those around them.

It is both strange and unfortunate that so many people protest war and the waste of human life, only to let the priceless wealth of human experience wither and die around them. Seek out the older people in your cities, towns, and neighborhoods. Take the time to visit them, to listen to what they have to say, and to learn from them. You will see why, throughout most of our history, it was the older people in the tribe who told the campfire stories that kept everyone else entertained.

Thomas Caldwell
Tokyo, July 1998

The Emperor's Court

As I LOOK BACK NOW, we were both kidding ourselves. Yet, the best way to deal with anxiety is to act as though everything is normal. We greeted the morning as if it were just another work day in the city. Midori and I got up at six-thirty, ate breakfast, and departed for the nearby train station for the hour-long ride to Tokyo.

We arrived at our office in Marunouchi about ten o'clock, and waited for the chauffeur-driven car to take us to the appointed place at the appointed time. Although I had attended similar events before, I couldn't help feeling a little tense and excited.

It was Friday, November 8, 1985. A major milestone in my life.

The car arrived on time and drove us to the Kasumigaseki district, the part of the city where one finds Tokyo's most important government buildings. We pulled up to the front entrance of the building that housed the Ministry of Foreign Affairs. Several people were there to greet us. They bowed deeply as our car came to a halt in front of them.

With all the officialdom and efficiency for which the Japanese are famous, we were whisked away to the Foreign Minister's drawing room and escorted to our seats.

There were twenty-four of us present, all sitting in a semi-square arrangement facing the center. A large bonsai pine tree graced the center of the opulent room that had hosted diplomats from all corners of the world.

The Deputy Foreign Minister, Mayumi Moriyama, Japan's first female Deputy Foreign Minister, announced the reason for our presence. Her message was simple, but spoken with the utmost elegance and tact. It was a very quiet and solemn ceremony, both dignified and systematic.

My name was the third one called. The deputy foreign minister announced that I was being presented with the Award of the Third Class Order of the Sacred Treasure for outstanding service to the Japanese people and nation. As Midori stood at my side, the minister handed me a formal proclamation and a medal in a small lacquer box. We bowed to each other. A lone photographer captured the moment.

After each of us had received our awards, we retired to a reception room and, as is the custom at such events, were served snacks and refreshments. After some nervous small talk, our escorts asked us to put on our decorations in preparation for a short visit to someone who lived down the street.

At one-thirty, they escorted us to several small buses and we set off towards our destination. During the trip, we all remained silent. Our convoy entered the palace grounds through the Sakuradamon gate of Tokyo's Imperial Palace and headed towards the home of the man whom General Douglas MacArthur had called "The First Gentleman of Japan."

As we emerged from the buses, chamberlains led us into the palace and through to the Grand Reception Hall. We walked side by side with our spouses, much like Japanese schoolchildren on their way to class.

The hall was empty like a Japanese Noh theater—no paintings, no decorations, nothing eye-catching to distract the visitors. With dignified precision, our handlers directed us to the places where we were to stand.

Then, at the other side of the room, the doors opened and the man whom many believe to be a direct descendant of the sun entered the room: The Emperor of Japan.

There was absolute silence. Not even the sound of someone breathing could be heard. The deafening quiet descended upon the room as he walked very slowly, with an aide beside him, to a stage at the front of the room.

Unlike the time that he had used the ancient language of the Imperial Court to tell the world that the worst war in human history was over, he congratulated us in ordinary Japanese. In a slow, deep voice, he told us that we had made significant contributions and service to the nation of Japan. He then wished us all good health.

As part of the ritual, a formal thank-you on behalf of the recipients was read to the Emperor. It thanked His Imperial Majesty for the honor that he had bestowed upon us, and promised that we would continue our good work.

We bowed before the man who was once worshiped as a god on earth. The bespectacled little man then left the stage and disappeared through the same doors from which he had come.

It was one of the most compelling moments of my life. As I stood there, watching the Emperor of Japan leave the room, I thought how only a few years can bring about so many changes in the life of a country and in the life of an individual. The man who had just thanked me was the head of state of the nation responsible for the Pearl Harbor deaths of several of my Annapolis classmates. Some of the best friends of my youth were entombed at the bottom of the ocean, courtesy of the navy he once commanded.

If, while standing on the bridge of my ship during the Second World War, a fellow sailor had told me that I would someday receive an award from the Emperor of Japan for promoting goodwill and friendship between his country and the United States, I would have thought him insane. However, time heals all wounds, and there is good in all people. That thought reverberated through my head that sunny autumn day.

We were escorted outside the palace where our group posed for photographs. After the cameras were finished, we climbed aboard the buses and returned to the Foreign Ministry for a reception. It was a wonderful party. The other recipients inundated Midori and me with questions about my life, background, and family—the usual small talk in which one engages at such times.

More pictures were taken and stories told. At six o'clock, the party ended and the events of the day were relegated to the domain of memory and scrapbooks. We climbed into our chauffeur-driven car and headed to see my longtime friend, Diet Representative Ganri Yamashita.

His eyes lit up when he greeted us at the door of his office. Yamashita-san had been a very good friend for many years. We had much in common, including our belief in the need for continued close ties between the armed forces of our two countries. We shared a lifelong love of the sea.

We stayed a short time. Dietmen are usually very busy people and one keeps them as friends by not forgetting that. Yamashita-san, Midori and I sat down and talked about our past accomplishments, and what the future promised. I cherish this moment as much as any other that occurred that day. After all, no one gets anywhere in life without being surrounded by good people.

After our visit, we then returned home. It had been a day as exhausting as it was memorable. Midori and I showered and went to bed. The next day, it would be back to business as usual. Being decorated by the Emperor had been pleasant, but Tokyo is a city where no one can afford to stand still for long.

As I began to fall asleep, one thought crossed my mind that put it all into perspective:

If you let it, a summer can last a lifetime.

The Call of the Sea

HAVE YOU EVER WONDERED WHY you were born when you were? Or, what your life would be like if you had come into the world at another time in history? What if you had been born during another age, in another nation, or to a different social class? It is a mind game that everybody plays and I am no exception.

We do not decide when or where we come into this world, so we have to work with what we are given. When we appear on the scene, we can only make the most of the situation and the talents with which we were born. Contrary to what one may think after reading a history book, the grass is not always greener at another point in time. Everybody who has ever lived was born during a time of interesting events and changes.

History is always happening. It is a never-ending process and we are witnesses to its consequences. Everyone on Earth, of every age and in every nation, is part of a never-ending chain of experiences and events that date back to the dawn of man. When we are born, our names are inscribed in the Bible of the human family. My name was written in that Bible on August 10, 1907, the date where my story, my link in the chain, begins.

If I could have chosen when I was to be born, and were given the opportunity to pick another time in history to come into this world, I would not do it. The twentieth century has been very eventful. I have witnessed many events and inventions, both wonderful and terrifying, and I would not trade the experience for anything.

The first decade of the twentieth century was a good time to be born. It was a simpler time—a much simpler time if one compares it to how complicated and rushed this century has become. In 1907, horses were still the primary form of transportation, and the "war" veterans who marched in Fourth of July parades (there was no Memorial Day yet) had served on battlefields named Bull Run, Lookout Mountain, and Gettysburg. The eldest son of Abraham Lincoln, Robert, was alive and thousands of Americans could recall a time when they had been considered "property," and "the war" was fought for their freedom.

When I came into this world, "Teddy" Roosevelt was President of the United States and his younger cousin, Franklin, had just passed the bar exam. In 1907, America was still an up-and-coming nation; some forty thousand men were laboring in subtropical heat to complete the Panama Canal; the RMS Titanic was not yet on the drawing board; the U.S. Army issued its first specifications for a military aircraft, and a young Robert Goddard worked on his doctoral dissertation, while dreaming of building a rocket that would fly men to the moon.

Personal bias aside, I would say that 1907 was a pretty good year.

My father, George Edgar Purdy, was a mining engineer by profession. Born in New York City in 1882, he served in the U.S. Navy during the later part of World War I aboard the battleship U.S.S. Oregon, the cruiser U.S.S. Cincinnati, and the destroyer U.S.S. Anthony. Afterwards, he served a couple of years as an officer in the Merchant Marines aboard a cargo ship called the Eastern Merchant.

When I was about sixteen, my father let me accompany him on a ten-day voyage from San Diego to San Francisco. The run included a stop in San Pedro, near Los Angeles. It was my first time aboard a ship of any size and I was thrilled. I hoped that my voyage would never end. In many ways, it never did.

My father was a good, honest man. Unfortunately, that is sometimes not enough. After his career at sea, things did not go well for him. He went from job to job and money was never plentiful. He married a woman who was both intelligent and industrious—a woman who had an interminable determination to succeed at whatever she decided to do.

My mother, Clara Irwin, was the daughter of a well-to-do doctor from Illinois. She met my father in Arizona while he was working as a mining engineer and she was teaching school. During her career, she held several jobs that required a strong-willed manager. Once, she even ran a hotel—an almost unheard of occupation at a time when women were not allowed to vote.

Mother, who was always up at the crack of dawn, lived a very austere and disciplined life. I may have inherited my love of the sea from my father, but I owe my successes to the mother who raised me and taught me valuable life lessons.

Having a father who was a sailor made it easy to follow the call of the sea. I was blessed to have been born at a time when adventure in foreign lands was a reality and, unlike today, not something only found in the movies or on television. As a young boy, if I wanted fun, I had no choice but to invent it myself.

As an only child, I also had to create my own siblings. With no brother or sister, I had to go out and find my own. For a brother, I found someone whom God himself could not have done a better job of bringing into my life.

Harry George Holloway and I became friends while we were students at a San Diego grammar school. We shared a taste for adventure, constantly dreaming of amazing things we would do and feats we would accomplish when, or if, we ever grew up.

It is one thing to dream about adventure. It is another thing to find it. Still, what young boys call adventurous, parents may call foolhardy and dangerous. A balance must be achieved between reality and what mom and dad will allow. Searching for something fun to do, of which parents will approve, can be as daunting a task as scaling Mount Everest or swimming across the English Channel.

Fortunately, persistence is the mother of discovery. One summer long ago, one that never really ended, I found a place where Harry and I learned about the beauty of the ocean and its dangers. This place was, almost literally, in my family's backyard.

Not too far from San Diego is a small group of islands, the Coronado Islands, that are Mexican territory. I discovered these magical foreign lands while working as a summer deck hand on a pleasure cruiser that made regular trips to the islands. For a young boy in his early teens, the Coronados were as exotic as the Galapagos were to Darwin.

At the beginning of the century, the Mexican government did not seem to care about the four small bodies of deserted land in the Pacific. Except for the sea birds and seals during the mating season, no one called the Coronados home. One of the four islands was called Dead Man's Island—an ominous name it earned from the silhouette of a pot-bellied man that it cast. Dead Man's Island! Harry and I could not think of a more adventurous place to spend our summer vacation (at least not one we could get to at our age).

As expected, it was not easy to convince our parents to let us camp alone for three weeks during the summer heat on a Mexican-held, desert island by the name of Dead Man. After all, Mexico was where Pancho Villa lived. Bandit raids were still a problem along the Texas border. What parents would be so foolish as to let their children spend the summer alone in a hostile foreign country? Harry and I prepared ourselves for our parents' refusal, but decided to give it our best shot.

Surprisingly, our mothers were more open to the idea than our fathers were. It still took some persuasion, but after my father visited the island to see where Harry and I wanted to spend our school break, he gave his approval. Both fathers wished us luck on our big adventure and helped us pack our gear. Provisioned like Stanley going to Africa, we borrowed a skiff from my employer, the cruise boat owner. The boat towed the skiff out to the island, and left us to fend for ourselves.

Our parents were not foolish. Although they knew we were on our own, the cruise boat returned three times a week and probably gave our family updates on our condition. The boat brought additional provisions and mail from our parents in San Diego, a distant twenty-five miles away.

Never in my life have I enjoyed myself so much or felt so free and alive as I did on Dead Man's Island. Picture an oval-shaped body of land less than a square mile in area, with a hundred-foot high ridge running from one end to the other; in the center, a crystal-clear cove with pure white sand covering the bottom; no people, no buildings, no sign of civilization; unchanged by the footprint of man for tens of thousands of years. It was our own secluded desert island. Instead of reading about distant and exotic lands, Harry and I were living on one.

"Desert island" is not the best term for a spot in the middle of the ocean with no human inhabitants. To me, a desert is a place without life. Dead Man's Island was full of life. Thousands of birds called the place home, the cove was full of leopard sharks, and all kinds of fish swam in the surrounding waters. Far from being a desert, Dead Man's Island was a paradise.

There were few safety concerns on the island. We slept outside, but marked the parameter of our campsite with a hemp rope to keep the tarantulas away. They covered the shore, but, for some strange reason, the large hairy spiders did not cross our hemp rope boundary.

Harry and I explored our little island home extensively. In one cave near the water, we made a frightening discovery that seemed to confirm an old sea tale often told by local fishermen.

Deep in the recesses of the cave, we found some very large bones. They were too big for a fish and not the kind that one would expect from a seal. We had heard stories of Chinese prisoners of Mexico whose captors left them on the island more than a century ago. We did not think anything of it until we discovered what may have been their tomb—their last shelter from the elements as they slowly wasted away on a desert island, thousands of miles from their homes.

We did not tell anyone of our find. We left the bones where we found them and wondered if they really were those of the Chinese who visited Mexico in the late-eighteenth century. I guess some mysteries are meant to remain unsolved.

Japanese and Italian fishermen used to anchor in the cove of our island for the night. Harry and I would row out to say hello, receiving live sardines to use as fishing bait in exchange for our efforts.

On one fishing trip, Harry and I took our little skiff a short distance from shore and cast out our line. At first, we did not think we would catch anything. Yet, one fish, a large rat-tailed stingray, took our sardine and went off like a shot, pulling us out to sea in the process.

It was a big fish but we, the two adventurers from San Diego, thought we could handle it. We tied the line to the bow of our skiff and hung on, thinking our catch would soon tire out.

Eventually it did, but so did we. After the ride, we made the terrifying discovery that we were over a mile away from the island. We cut the line and started back to shore. I took the starboard and Harry took the port oar, as we began to row for our lives.

As always, we made a good team, but we were far from shore and fright has a way of sapping one's strength, even if one is an indestructible youth. By the time reached the shore, we were exhausted, hungry and scared. We collapsed on the beach with barely enough strength to secure the boat.

It was not until much later that we came to fully realize how much trouble that fishing trip could have caused us. That far out, we were dangerously close to getting caught in a current that would have swept us to the middle of the Pacific. In the days before the Coast Guard's widespread use of aircraft, we could have disappeared without a trace. The thought scared into both of us the power of nature and the realization of our own mortality.

Growing up, nothing was more adventurous, nothing was more mysterious, and nothing was more dangerous than the blue-green monster, also known as the ocean. During that summer, my brother and I learned more about life and about the world that awaited us than we could have ever learned at school.

Our three weeks of adventure ended too soon. Harry and I returned to our home port of San Diego and greeted our parents with more affection than they probably expected.

As I fell asleep in my own bed for the first time in weeks, safe at home with my family, I found myself pleased with the success of my adventure. However, I was in far less of a hurry to grow up.

A Walk on the Beach

As boys slowly become men, the hurry to grow up is replaced with the worry of an unknown future.

However, at some point, the fear of the future is replaced by the self-confidence needed to take on the world. For many people, including myself, this confidence emerges when one encounters an individual—a special individual—who becomes a role model.

About the time high school graduation approaches, one is faced with the inevitable: adulthood. No longer is it one's job to prepare for life, but rather to learn to deal with its problems and challenges. It is at this time when boys tend to hang out with older men, in the search for a mentor.

For me, that fateful event came on a day when a few friends and I were at Ocean Beach, near San Diego. While enjoying the warm sand and surf, we encountered a tall, lanky guy sitting on the sand all alone. He gazed over the ocean, seemingly deep in thought. His eyes were those of someone who was both excited and worried, but determined not to let either emotion get the better of him.

Being curious kids, with nothing better to do with our time, and lacking any respect for the guy's privacy, we matter-of-factly walked up to him and struck up a conversation. He got to his feet and seemed happy for the company, probably as bored as we were. Our group spent a good part of the day together. When the sun told us to move on we arranged to get together again.

Our little group met about two or three times a week. Our new friend, who was called "Slim," turned out to be a great guy to hang out with. He was in his mid-twenties, close enough in age to be a friend and old enough to be interesting, so we got along with him just fine.

During small talk, Slim told us that he was a mail pilot from the Midwest and was having a special airplane built at a nearby factory. He also said a group of men was paying a lot of money for the plane, and, if everything went well he would be able to fly it all the way to Europe.

At first, we thought Slim was joking. A nonstop flight to Europe? Many stories in the newspapers were about people trying to be first to fly across the Atlantic, some dying in the process. Nobody had ever done it before, and we thought that people planning such an adventure would not hang around on the beach with adolescents.

We asked our newfound buddy if we could see his custom-built plane. In the 1920s, aircraft were still novelties. To have a chance to see an airplane fly, let alone to see how one is built, was a real treat. Slim agreed and we made a date to meet at the Ryan Aircraft Factory, located on the salt flats between San Diego and Point Loma.

Today, it may seem hard to believe that aircraft manufacturing was once a cottage industry. Aviation was something new—really new. Commercial passenger planes were, excuse the pun, just getting off the ground. In many small towns across America, an airplane flying overhead would be the big event for the week. In 1926, visiting an aircraft factory was like visiting Cape Canaveral and watching the Space Shuttle being built.

Slim greeted us outside the front gate at the appointed time. It did not look like a place from which something as graceful as an airplane would come. It seemed more like a machine shop, common to every U.S. city of the time. It smelled of grease and welded metal.

Slim's plane was almost finished. As it was explained to us, the engineers were conducting weight tests by placing bags of sand inside.

Most of Slim's explanation of how everything worked was over our heads. Nevertheless, we found the whole process fascinating. Our group made several visits to Slim's factory over a period of a few weeks while the engineers were putting the finishing touches on his plane.

One day while I was visiting Slim at the Ryan factory, he showed me the inside of the cockpit. The instrument panel was a maze of knobs and gauges whose use or purpose I could not even fathom. The pilot's seat was not what one would expect in a state-of-the-art aircraft. It was a small wicker chair that Slim said had been donated by a local company that specialized in household wicker furniture.

The seat folded forward, for some reason I never did figure out, and underneath it was the floor. It was not made of metal like those found in the aircraft of today, but of a thin woven fabric. Slim lifted up the seat and, in a matter-of-fact sort of way, handed me a pen, asking if I would like to sign my name on the fuselage under the seat.

I do not know why he made the offer, but it seemed to me that he thought it would bring him good luck. I said, "sure," and signed my name, "George I. Purdy," on the exposed floor, wishing him the best of luck.

About a week later, Slim took off in his brand-new plane, "The Spirit of St. Louis," for the East Coast and, as it would turn out, for the history books. I never met or corresponded with Charles Lindbergh again, but I did follow his life and career with a great deal of interest until his death in 1974.

Lindbergh, like all of us, had his ups and downs. Some events, like the kidnapping and murder of his infant son, must have devastated him. Other events, like greeting the Apollo XI astronauts on the deck of an aircraft carrier after their return from the moon, must have been exhilarating. I didn't realize until many years later the impact my chance meeting with Charles Lindbergh had on my life and on my way of thinking.

Later that year, as I read about his historic trip across the Atlantic, and his exploits around the world, I thought about how ordinary he had seemed sitting on the beach in San Diego and staring out to sea.

It proved something that I had known since Harry and I had spent time on Dead Man's Island: if you set your mind to it, truly anything is possible.

As Slim embarked upon his lifetime of adventure, I set to work on plans for my own.

Uncle's Gift

THROUGHOUT OUR LIVES, we all experience brief moments wherein we find ourselves sitting at a very specific place and at a very specific time contemplating our future. It usually happens for only a few minutes, but we look back on those moments for the rest of our lives. We ask the Fates what the future holds and then we wait for it to happen.

For me, that moment was during an afternoon in 1919. I was growing up quickly. The summertime innocence of childhood would soon give way to adult responsibilities. There would soon be many decisions that would affect the rest of my days.

I was sitting in the living room of my family's home in San Diego. A light rain was falling outside, a rare event in southern California. For no particular reason, I just sat on our sofa, gazed out the window, and wondered what the future held in store for me.

It was a Saturday and my father was home from his latest voyage. The next day he would be heading back to sea. He quietly walked into our small living room and sat down, gazing out the window for a silent moment before turning his attention to me.

My father was more somber than usual, leading me to think that he had something important to tell me. Like most boys, I thought that some past mischief of mine had been discovered.

In my father's hand was a small, felt-covered box. As he held it out, he told me in a strong but gentle voice that his brother, my uncle, had died. Before he passed away, he had instructed that I be given one of his most prized possessions.

I had never met my uncle, so there were no tears or sadness on my part. However, receiving a gift from someone unknown, especially someone deceased, was a new and creepy experience.

He handed me the small box and I opened it. Inside was a large gold ring bearing the image of a double-headed eagle. A fair-sized diamond was set in the center.

My father explained to me that his brother had been a Freemason. As he had no sons, and all Freemasons must be males, he wanted me to have the ring.

Wow, I thought! A diamond ring! Just like the ones pirates and buccaneers used to fight and die for! I could not wait to tell my friends. However, as I went to try on my new treasure, my father quickly stopped me, saying that I had not yet earned the "right" to wear it.

He proceeded to explain that I had many things to study and do before I would be allowed to wear the ring on my finger. Perplexed, but having a healthy respect for the unknown, I promised to never wear the ring until it "was time." Following our talk, I added the small black box to my growing collection of treasures, where it remained for many, many years.

Such was my first exposure to an organization, and to a philosophy, that would have a profound impact on my life. The gift was from my unknown uncle, William B. Purdy, who had become a 32nd Degree Scottish Rite Mason on January 17, 1919 in the State of New York.

Freemasonry, for those who are unfamiliar with it, is a very old fraternal organization that dates back to the stonemason guilds of medieval Europe. Quite simply, the Masons are a fellowship of men who do what they can to better society. Some of the greatest men of the modern era were Freemasons: Benjamin Franklin, George Washington, Paul Revere, Theodore "Teddy" Roosevelt, Winston Churchill, Neil Armstrong, Charles Lindbergh, and Douglas MacArthur.

What attracts people's attention when the word "Freemason" is mentioned, is its reputation as clandestine and secretive. The organization does have secrets. However, these "secrets" are neither sensational nor particularly interesting. The Freemasonry secrets are, for want of a better term, symbolic. They are a method of teaching a very important life lesson: a man must be trustworthy to his family and to his friends. One of the best ways to deem a man trustworthy is to see how well he keeps a secret.

One would think that it would be a privilege and an honor to be associated with such a fraternity. It is an honor, but not everyone thinks so. Throughout much of its history, Freemasonry has been attacked because of its so-called "secrets." Some governments and religions have persecuted Masons, accusing the fraternity of subversion, treason, assassination—even witchcraft and demon worship. Freemasons have been put to death at times, even during this century, because of these falsehoods.

My adoptive home of Japan is no exception to anti-Masonic hysteria. Before World War II, Japan forbade its citizens to legally become Freemasons. Foreigners who were members of Masonic lodges in Japan were tolerated, but watched with great suspicion by the authorities. After the outbreak of the Pacific War, authorities arrested members of the fraternity and seized their possessions. Some were tortured by the notorious Kempetai who hoped that they would reveal the Freemasonry "secrets." This nonsense even extended to the regalia used in Masonic rituals being put on display in Tokyo department stores, alongside graphic descriptions of their "evil uses."

Following the war, General Douglas MacArthur, himself a Mason, ordered all property that had been taken from the fraternity to be returned. Land was also sold to the Freemasons in Japan that, ironically, had belonged to the Imperial Navy. Today, the Grand Lodge of Japan occupies the site where the "Suikosha," the Imperial Japanese Navy's Officers Club, once stood. It is in the center of Tokyo, next to the landmark Tokyo Tower.

Controversy aside, Freemasonry is a systematic method of accepting good men, and making these good men even better. It is not just a group of men who get together to wear fancy aprons and funny little hats. It is a way of life. While not a religion, Freemasonry imposes a moral code upon its members that promotes industry, charity, and the taking care of one's family. In short, Freemasonry is for those who are honest and responsible. Far from being worshipers of the devil, some of the Masons I have met are the closest I will ever come to meeting saints.

After receiving my uncle's gift, I kept an interest in Freemasonry, but did not act on this interest until I met several Masons at my place of employment in Texas in 1938. I applied for membership and was accepted as an Entered Apprentice in El Paso Lodge Number 130.

I remained active in my lodge for awhile but, as the clouds of World War II loomed on the horizon, there was little time for involvement. It was not until almost twenty years later, in 1958, that I again became an active member, this time in Tokyo Lodge Number 2, under the jurisdiction of the newly-formed Grand Lodge of Japan. In 1964, I joined another Japanese lodge called Harmony, of which I became Master in 1969.

In 1963, I received the Scottish Rite Degrees in the Tokyo Scottish Rite Bodies. Almost half a century since a young boy received a ring as a gift from a stranger, he was ready to place it on his finger.

I continued to be active in Scottish Rite Masonry and was the first person to become Master of all four bodies. In 1960, I received the honor of Knight Commander of the Court of Honour. In 1967, I became the recipient of the 33rd degree Inspector General Honorary in Washington, D.C.

All men have pillars that support the structure of their lives. For me, the one on which I have always relied, and the one that will be with me for the rest of my days, is the fraternity of Freemasons. I do not think that I would have gotten as far as I have without them.

My interest in Freemasonry turned out to be the greatest gift I ever received. Amazingly, it came from a man I never knew. Yet somehow, for reasons that will always remain a mystery, he knew me.

Anchors Away

IT HAS BEEN A RECRUITING PHRASE USED BY EVERY NAVY of every country since seagoing ships were first built, for the simple fact that it is true: "Join the Navy and see the world."

There was never a doubt in my mind that after high school I would head straight to sea. The Navy beckoned and I followed. When I was eighteen, I wanted nothing more than to get into the U.S. Naval Academy at Annapolis and enter the Navy as an officer.

Unfortunately, in the late 1920s, the entire U.S. military, especially the Navy, was trying to thin out its ranks. There were too many officers and, given the congressional budget cut of such "extravagances," the Navy Department had no choice but to limit the number of people it accepted. There were more graduates of Annapolis than there were positions to be filled. Getting an appointment was not easy, and for me it turned out to be impossible.

However, there was more than one way to get into the academy. I learned of a program where some one hundred sailors a year, fifty from the East Coast and fifty from the West Coast, could get into Annapolis if they passed the entrance examinations. Given the number of sailors who wanted to go to Annapolis, it seemed a long shot. Nevertheless, I decided to give it a try. I joined the Navy as an enlisted man and became a seaman on June 30, 1926. I reported for duty at the training station in San Diego.

The pre-World War II Navy was, in a word, family. It was a very small, close-knit organization which, compared with the U.S. military shopping mall of today, was a small town general store. The military strategy was not to maintain readiness in case of war, but to do what was necessary to keep the system working. In those days, governments still had a lot of time to plan for a war. As a result, funds were limited and the technology was not always cutting-edge. We wore jumpers, carried our possessions in sea bags, and slept in hammocks. We were not too different from our predecessors of a century earlier.

If you were in the Navy back then, everybody knew it. Sailors were not allowed to wear civilian clothes, even when off duty. However, most of us had lockers at the local YMCA where we kept some civilian clothes and a tailor-made uniform. The "tailor-mades," as we called them, fit a lot better than the baggy standard issues in which we worked. When we came ashore, it was down to the YMCA to change clothes before a night on the town.

The pre-war Navy was a much simpler institution than it is today. It was so simple that an officer was expected to know everything about running a ship. He had to learn a wide variety of skills. Knowledge of radio, navigation, and engineering had to be learned as one moved up through the ranks.

Due to the relatively simple technology of the time, these tasks were not as difficult as they sound. Today, the amount of training needed to run even the smallest part of a ship requires a specialist. Generalists are a thing of the past.

After I went through basic training, the first ship I was assigned to was the battleship U.S.S. California. Excitement is not the word for what I felt the day I came aboard. A battleship was *the* ship to be on at the time. No other type of ship was considered more exciting, or safer, to serve on. The aircraft carrier was still viewed as an expensive, experimental oddity by most of the world's navies—except for the Imperial Navy of Japan.

Our attitude towards aircraft carriers would prove to be one of the most serious strategic errors in naval history. Fifteen years later, at a place called Pearl Harbor, the U.S.S. California would be on the receiving end of that judgement error.

They assigned me to the California for only a month, after which they told me I had qualified to take the Naval Academy Preparatory Class, or NAPC, at San Diego. My chance to enter Annapolis had arrived.

As it turned out, getting accepted into the class was the easy part. The competition in the program was intense. The NAPC was seven months of grueling classroom instruction, probably only surpassed in its intensity by medical school. *Everything* was covered: English, mathematics, science, social studies and military subjects of all kinds—the works. Our instructors tested us regularly and rigorously. Every week, those who fell to the bottom of the class were cut. The system was designed not so much to prepare us for the Annapolis examination, but to eliminate those who did not have a chance. It was survival of the most seaworthy.

During the program, I became friends with two other Annapolis hopefuls: Willis Manning ("Tommy") Thomas and Herb Jukes. They had also joined the Navy in the hopes of getting into the Naval Academy. The three of us worked hard together. When not in class, we studied together, testing each other until the lights went out at night.

I also met an instructor who would later become a lifelong friend. He was a young lieutenant by the name of Benny Decker and was OIC (Officer in Charge) of our class. The good-natured Decker, who always had something positive to say about everyone, would later become an admiral, playing a role in the occupation of Japan.

After seven months, all three of us were still in the program and our decisive moment, the final examination, was upon us. The exam was to occur over a three-day period. There were six tests in all, one administered in the morning and another in the afternoon. A candidate had to pass all six with flying colors or it was back to the ranks.

We arrived at the examination room directly after breakfast. Lt. Decker was there with several ensigns to assist him. The class was told to be seated and to wait. After a few minutes, we started looking around the room, wondering when our test papers would be distributed.

Suddenly, a mail orderly strode into the room carrying a bundle. The ensigns immediately closed and locked all the doors. The orderly opened the package, gave the contents to Lt. Decker, and sat in a corner.

To ensure that nobody could get a peek at the exams beforehand, the Navy arranged for a courier from Annapolis to arrive at the base just before the exams were scheduled to begin. The package was given to the mail orderly who carried it the classroom straightaway. They ordered him to remain with the contents and to never let them leave his sight.

Each separate examination was two hours in length, not a minute more. If you did not finish, that was too bad. When the time was up, the ensigns immediately collected the test papers and gave them to the orderly. He placed them in a package, proceeding to seal it with string, ribbon and wax. Then, he strode out of the room with an air of importance that one would expect from someone marching out of the Oval Office.

The same order of events occurred over the next two days. Packages sent from the other side of the country arrived in our classroom at a specific minute. Up until that time, I had never seen a finer example of military precision.

Weeks of anxiety followed. Nobody told us when we would hear the results of our labors. Anyone who has ever known the pain of waiting for long periods of time will know what I mean. Not passing meant back to the ranks and, more than likely, never becoming an officer.

One night, while asleep in our barracks, we were awakened by a student who seemed to have gone mad. He was jumping up and down while kicking most of us out of our hammocks. The test results had arrived!

We tumbled out of our hammocks and ran to the main gate where the list of those accepted was to be found. The early morning hours were actually a blessing; if anyone had been so unlucky as to have been caught between us and the gate, they would have been trampled.

Upon reaching the guardhouse at the gate, trying to catch my breath, I asked the guard on duty if my name was on the list. He looked at me as if I were drunk. "Is my name on the list?" I begged him. "Is my name on the list?" I was desperate for a response.

"First, I think you better tell me your name," he answered, trying to hide a thin smile.

"George I. Purdy," I blurted out.

"Yup," he said. "Your name's here."

A howl of joy echoed across Southern California. Then Tommy asked the guard if his name was on the list. "Yes" was again the response. Tommy proceeded to bounce around like a rubber ball.

Then Herb, who had worried incessantly since the examinations, asked if he was going to Annapolis. The guard carefully eyeballed the clipboard in front of him, looked at Herb, and slowly shook his head. Herb had not passed. Tommy and I stopped our personal celebrations. Herb put his face in his hands and began to sob uncontrollably.

Never in my life, before or since, have I ever experienced such a torrent of mixed emotions as I did walking from the main gate to our barracks. After a lot of work, and a lot of risk, the U.S. Naval Academy had accepted me. I was going to Annapolis. My dream had come true.

Yet, Herb was not coming with us. He had worked just as hard as the rest of us, but he did not make it. He was heading back to the fleet as an enlisted man. His dream of being an officer in the Navy was shattered.

Tommy and I put our arms around our friend as we slowly walked back to the barracks. We did not know what to say or what to do. Sadness, mixed with happiness, is one of the most bitter of wines.

A few days later, almost exactly a year after entering the Navy, I received my orders to head for Annapolis. I was to be enrolled in the class of 1931. All the hard work had paid off. I was on my way.

As for Herb, he eventually followed Tommy and me to the Academy. Not being one to give up, he reapplied to the program and repeated the seven months of hell. The next year, he passed the exams and was accepted into the Annapolis class of 1932. Herb went on to have a distinguished career in the Navy and retired as a captain. Once again, I saw proof that anything is possible if you set your mind to it.

I knew that a lot of work was still ahead of me, but I had gambled and won. In just four years, I would be an ensign in the United States Navy. My future would be secure, challenging and, most of all, full of adventure. I would be sailing the seven seas and, just as the recruiters had promised, seeing the world.

Nevertheless, as I would soon learn, a lifetime is a lot like a day: it never goes exactly as you plan.

Annapolis

UNLIKE THE COLD WAR-ERA MACHINE that the United States Armed Forces later became, the Army, Navy and Marines (there was no Air Force yet) of the early part of the century resembled a community college more than a superpower in the making. World War I was a quickly fading memory. The "bad guys" of the world seemed to have been vanquished (the Soviet Union was not taken seriously at the time), making way for a future of sunshine and fun.

Money was plentiful in the late 1920s. Everybody seemed to have lots of it. Making it, spending it, and then making more of it was the pulse of the country. It was an era of fine clothes, fast cars, singing, dancing and travel. To many people, it was just as Hollywood now depicts it—a carefree time of fun and games for all.

Much of this attitude spilled over to the public and military sectors. Although he only gave Annapolis midshipmen a small allowance, Uncle Sam provided our meals and other essentials, which gave us a reasonable amount of disposable income. During the off-hours, we had fun just like everyone else.

Since the country was at peace, and the thought of another war was far from everyone's minds, especially those who sat in Congress, the competition to get into the Naval Academy was highly intense. Perhaps more so than it ever was or will be. The Navy needed very few high level officers in peacetime, so we all dreamed of becoming the top of the class, and having the luxury of not worrying about our future. We were all going to spend our lives in the Navy. After all, we had made it to Annapolis.

Many of the rituals, pranks and jokes for which military academies have become famous were prevalent at the time. Still, nothing brutal ever transpired. Freshmen, known as plebes, always had to address a higher classman as "sir," and had to perform many of the chores around the living quarters. The shining of boots and shoes was the most common, while sitting on a toilet seat on a cold morning to warm it up for one's "boss" was also part of one's duty.

It was a very innocent, civilized time. Officers were trained to be gentlemen and acted the part day in and day out. The Naval ceremony of life could best be compared with priesthood. Few were chosen to go to Annapolis, so those few had to be the best the nation had to offer. None of us wanted to disgrace the honor bestowed upon us.

Unlike the other branches of the service, the Navy has always been more than a group of well-trained warriors. The Navy was, and in many ways still is, the first line of a nation's defense. A key part of any defensive strategy involves a great deal of diplomacy. In the days before long-haul aircraft, satellite communication and the other technological marvels we have come to take for granted, a Navy captain had a great deal of responsibility to the country he served. He could not easily contact his superior and await instructions from the State Department. He *was* the State Department. A ship at sea had the power to take any action deemed necessary to protect U.S. interests or the lives of its citizens. In an emergency, a ship captain might have to deal directly with a foreign government or with its military. If he were not careful, he could start a war. If he were clever, he could prevent one. A Naval officer could also be called in to act as a mediator or arbitrator in some distant country, in a role similar to that of today's American diplomats. All the contingencies required individuals of the highest training, not only in war, but in the arts of civilization.

At Annapolis, they taught us everything a top-level university would, and then some. Our studies included all the sciences, politics, liberal arts, languages and histories of the other people of the world. They designed the curriculum so that we would be as much at home at a diplomatic soiree in Paris, as we would be on the bridge of a ship on the open sea.

At the time, the United States was considered an up-and-coming power. Our military and naval powers were nothing like those of the British. We were a nation of upstarts, considered a bit backward by the rest of the world. However, in the 1920s, the world's naval battles were fought with words and wit instead of guns. Technology and weapons did not rule the world; gentlemen did.

After years of hard work, I had finally made it. I was a Naval officer in training at Annapolis. I was to graduate in 1931. A fairy tale life of an officer in the United States Navy awaited me—or so I thought.

In late 1929, the Roaring Twenties came to a screeching halt. Although the stock market crash and the beginning of the era known as the Great Depression did not directly affect the military, it did affect those who paid the bills: Congress.

In budget-cutting moves, much like those imposed at the end of the Cold War in the early 1990s, the War Department was told to scale back on what little it was actually doing. In lean times, be it business or government, the first thing to go is the people.

Anyone who has ever been in the military knows how quickly rumors spread. At first, when news of the problems with the civilian economy surfaced, none of the second year midshipmen like myself were particularly worried. If anything, we were all happy that we had chosen the careers we had. We reassured ourselves that none of the problems facing ordinary people would affect us.

Reality proved us wrong. There was to be a scaling back of all branches of the armed services. Recruitment of enlisted personnel was to be drastically reduced, as well as the number of officers needed to command them. Early retirement was offered to many. With stormy seas ahead, few people in the Navy wanted to leave. The need for new officers was almost nonexistent and would continue to be so for the foreseeable future. If Uncle Sam did not need us, why should he pay for our education?

As the months passed, the rumor mill started to turn out tales of doom and gloom that had a great deal of truth to them. Only in my second year, I was in the wrong place at the wrong time. In a very unceremonious letter, delivered to me in my dormitory, the academy told me that I was to leave at the end of the term. No apologies. No regrets.

It was a time of great disappointment and sadness that, even today, I still do not like to think about. I was in my early twenties and what little adulthood I had experienced had been spent on my career in the Navy, my life at sea. I had dedicated my young life to it. I had dreamed about it, lived it day in and day out, and committed my existence—my soul—to it.

Yet in spite of it all, the Navy did not want me. I had become unnecessary and insignificant. Like a character in a Charles Dickens tale, I was an expense listed on the ledger of some cold-hearted, bespectacled bureaucrat in nearby Washington. I was an item to be crossed out with a red pencil, like too much toilet paper or too many truck tires. An American Scrooge had robbed me of everything for which I had lived. I thought I would never return to the sea again.

Although others had been turned out as well, and were facing the same difficulties, I was more alone than at any other time in my life, before or since. Tears came easy, as did anger. Fights broke out among some of my classmates, but I avoided conflict. I suffered alone, taking walks around campus and the surrounding countryside. Dreams, I discovered, were everything. Dreams were what lead to reality. Take them away, and nothing exists in one's life.

Besides the emotion of the time, there was the worry of how to live. The Depression was quickly approaching and I had never held a real job in the private sector. I would not only be competing for work with other unemployed sailors, but with *millions* of unemployed men with far more experience than I had. No matter how I looked at it, the future was dark. There was no Social Security system at the time and no government welfare of which to speak.

The few charity groups were soon overwhelmed by the masses in need of food. Not only were my dreams gone, but my very survival was in doubt.

Throughout history, old sailors, used up and forgotten, dying at the side of the road, have been a common sight. I worked hard to keep this image out of my mind, but with little success. As the day that I was to enter the "real world" approached, seemingly unprepared for it, I began to worry so much that I was unable to eat. I hated falling asleep at night because it meant I would have to awaken to inescapable uncertainty.

The upper classmen, who would soon be graduating as officers, treated us with a lot more sympathy than we desired. It made some of us feel worse, like we really did not matter anymore and were no longer worth the effort to order around.

One day, not long before graduation, one of the seniors who had been especially hard on us approached me in the hallway. He looked me straight in the eye, and held out his hand.

It was a tradition called "spooning." The act of shaking hands with a lower classman meant that you were no longer considered beneath him, and no longer had to address him as "sir." You were an equal. It was not plebe and upper classman, it was comrades in arms.

It was also an act of kindness at a time when it was sorely needed. Still, being "spooned on" meant you deserved it. It was never done for sympathy. Your hard work had been recognized and shown respect. It was understood that, most of all, your courage was respected.

Courage? I was scared out of my wits. I had no idea what awaited me outside the Navy. There was very little in my situation that brought the word courage to mind. Still, I shook hands with the upperclassman. We both smiled, he gave me a snappy salute that I returned, and then we went about our business.

Over the next few days, it finally dawned on me what it all meant. He would graduate and become a Naval officer, one of the few lucky ones who would not have to worry about making a living or having enough to eat in the coming years. I, on the other hand, would be on my own. My future, a struggle to be sure, was anything but certain. He would have no such worries, no such concerns, and no such challenge in his life.

Challenge? I began to dwell on the thought while lying awake one night. The realization slowly came to me that what awaited outside was not so much a struggle as it was a challenge. My life after the Navy was an obstacle to be overcome, not very different from the many that had stood in my way on the road to Annapolis. Challenge was why I chose the life I did. It was what drove me since the time I was a boy dreaming of the sea. I had readily accepted challenge in the past, why should it now be any different?

It was true that the upperclassman who spooned on me would have an easier life than I would. He would have the life of which I had been dreaming. Yet, I would have a more formidable challenge, one that he might never experience. If he ever went into a great naval battle, his would be a ship and many men to command. In my battle with the growing chaos on American streets, all I would have to call upon would be my wits and what I had learned up to that point in time. I began to feel very strange about things. Could it be that he envied me? Did he envy the fact that I would be able to prove myself a success or failure against an enemy far more formidable than any that had ever sailed the seas? That enemy would be myself.

Perspective comes with experience. It might seem obvious now, but it did not at the time. Before my last day at Annapolis, I had stopped agonizing over that which I could not control and I started to plan for things I could. A new challenge awaited me, and all challenges hold uncertainty.

It was 1929. The Navy had no place for me. Although nobody suspected it at the time, America would soon descend into economic and social chaos. Millions would look for work and millions would be hungry—millions who had better odds of making it than I did. If ever there was a time for challenge, it was then.

My earlier dreams were quickly disappearing beneath the waves. It was either go down with the ship or survive to fight another day. I held my breath, closed my eyes, and jumped into the great unknown.

Alchemy

YES, IT IS TRUE. All of the stories are accurate. The late 1920s to early 1930s was a lousy time to be job-hunting.

For those who did not live through it, the Great Depression was as bad as the history books describe it to be. The basic necessities of life, food and shelter, being at the top of the list, were never taken for granted during those dark years.

The dream was over. I was out of the Navy. After saying goodbye to my friends at Annapolis, I packed up what few possessions I owned and headed to the nearest big city with which I was familiar: Baltimore.

In spite of the free-spending attitude of recent years, I had managed to save some money. It was not much, but enough to survive for at least a few weeks. After a bit of a search, I found a family who was renting out a room in their house for a modest price. They were pleasant folks and, like so many others, were doing what they could to get by. Renting out a spare room in one's house was a common way to help make ends meet. Since I was a recent Annapolis midshipman, far from my home in California, they treated me better than the average tenant. In retrospect, it was my first successful business deal.

As expected, I was silently terrified that my money would run out. Not wanting to live on the street, I took the first job I could find. I cut my teeth in the business world as a door-to-door salesman for the Fuller Brush Company.

At the time, I knew nothing of sales, or even the general principles of business. I was given a suitcase full of brushes and told that for each brush I sold, I would earn a certain amount of money.

It sounded simple enough, and lots of people need brushes. So, with all the enthusiasm I could muster, I hit the streets.

Given how little money people had at the time, every penny was guarded jealously by the head of the household: the housewife. Most of my prospects were women who scraped to keep food on the table. Having doors slammed in one's face by the dozen is a very sober introduction to the world of commerce—and a great way to learn to deal with rejection.

Unfortunately, many of the housewives had far more business savvy than I did. Most detected my naiveté and they took full advantage of it. A prospective brush customer often asked me how much my commission was. Not knowing any better, I would tell her. She would then ask me if I was willing to "split" my commission if she bought the brush. Thinking half a commission is better than nothing, I would agree. We made the transaction and, after doing the same thing about a dozen times, I found myself to be the only Fuller Brush salesman in Baltimore who was losing money.

After working for Fuller for about a month, I began to seriously doubt my future in the brush business. Money was running low and I was getting desperate. Many other people were in the same boat. The Depression had not yet completely arrived, but most people had a premonition of the future: bleak. Parties were common, not because people wanted to celebrate, but because they needed a place to drink (Prohibition was still enforced) and a venue to make contacts for their latest deals or scams.

At a party held at the home of a friend of a friend, I met an Annapolis graduate whom I had briefly known a few years before. He graduated from the academy the same year I came in. However, since the Navy had been reducing the number of officers on its payroll, he never received his commission and was turned out just like I was.

While swapping sea stories about what we thought were the good old days, the subject of earning a living came up. I told my former upperclassman that selling brushes was not my forte and that I was, like millions of other Americans, looking for a job.

It was then that my luck began to change. He told me he had landed a job with the American Smelting & Refining Company at their Baltimore Copper Works. I was told that business was quite good and that the company might soon be looking for some more workers.

Copper refining? Metals? I told him I had no experience in the field. Why would they want me?

"Why wouldn't they? If anything, your time at Annapolis proves you are disciplined and not afraid to take on responsibility," he told me with a bit of sarcasm. "Good people are always in demand, George, and you are good people." He told me that he would check into things at his office and I was asked to come down and meet with him later in the week.

The interview with the heads of AS&R took only a few minutes. They hired me on the spot. They offered good pay, and asked me to report to work as soon as possible. Although I knew next to nothing about metals, my career in the industry had begun.

My turn of luck and life had happened so fast that I did not know what to expect. The plant was an enormous structure and I found it as intimidating as a battleship—even more so because I knew my way around a battleship and knew what it did. I had never even thought about the metals business.

I was initially assigned to the refinery's tank house as a trainee. It was a cavernous building wherein the electrolytic refining of copper took place. Over the next several months, I learned some of the ins and outs of copper and other metals: how they were produced, what their uses were, and their importance in different industries. It was not only good, steady pay, it was downright interesting work—almost magical. I spent a great deal of my spare time reading everything I could about metals and their production processes.

I buried myself in every history book or technical manual on the subject that I could find. I had found my calling.

Although I was thankful for having a steady, well-paying job, after working for the company for a little less than a year, I began to look for something else. I had been promoted and was given a raise. However, I had begun to realize that in order to get any higher up on the corporate ladder, my immediate supervisor would either have to quit or die—the latter being the only possibility during the increasingly worsening economy.

I had made some contacts in the metals business, and had heard through the grapevine that the Nichols Copper Company was building a new refinery in El Paso, Texas. They needed all sorts of people to staff the new facility. I had only been in the business for eleven months, but I thought I would give it a try. So I took a few days off and went to Long Island, New York to visit the company's headquarters.

I had been talking with the head of the El Paso plant project for less than an hour when he offered me a managerial position at the new facility. I never knew exactly why he hired me. All I could find out was that he felt my time at Annapolis and my one year in the industry was sufficient. I immediately accepted the position. Not believing my luck, I gave my notice at AS&R and started packing for Texas.

I traveled to my new job—my new life—with two other men who were to be working at the new plant. None of us had ever been to Texas before. We spent most of our time on the train talking about the future. We were all young, excited and ambitious.

The plant was still being completed when we arrived. It was a fascinating experience to be part of a massive construction project, even if one just sat on the sidelines and watched. The workers were building my plant, my future. A year ago, I was desperate and trying to sell brushes to housewives. Now, I was part of a major industrial enterprise.

Texas—the climate, the people and the town of El Paso—agreed with me. It was a very pleasant place and still is today. It was a small town where most people knew each other. Being close to the Mexican border, it also reminded me of San Diego, without the ocean.

Nichols Copper was under contract to a company called Phelps-Dodge Corporation to electrolytically refine smelted copper that they were producing in Arizona. The companies had a close relationship and would eventually merge in 1935. Initially, I held a relatively low position at the plant, but luck held out. Almost a year to the day after I joined Nichols, the refinery's department head was let go. They made his assistant the new department head and, to my surprise, they gave me the job as his new assistant. It was my duty to effectively run the place on a day-to-day basis.

Life became better than I could have ever hoped for just over a year ago. I was becoming well-to-do and well known in the local community. El Paso was where I came of age. It is where I became "somebody." I met a young woman named Mary Robinson and after the usual courtship ritual, we married. We moved into a company house near the plant. It was a very nice, quiet and peaceful life. At El Paso, I spent some of the happiest, most carefree years I would ever experience.

If you look for something you may never find it, but if you stop looking and wait for awhile, it just may find you. I did not think about what I wanted to do for a career. Given the circumstances, to do so would have been impractical. I went into metallurgy because it was what was available at the time. In retrospect, I could have gone into other fields and done just as well. However, there are just as many fields wherein I could have done badly. I took the opportunity presented to me and made the most of it.

Throughout the 1930s, I worked at the El Paso plant for Phelps-Dodge. While many in the United States were looking for work, I held a comfortable, well-paying position. My life in the Navy became a fading memory, like something experienced in another lifetime. Still, the dream, which had become a fantasy, never really left me. I sometimes thought of the sea, the ships, and the men who traveled on them. I thought about the life I once dreamed would be mine. Although I was happy, there was the adventurous boy inside of me who never wanted to come home from the deserted island in the middle of nowhere.

I went on with my work and with my career. Although I had my fantasy, I was content with the life I had chosen.

However, the world continued to be a dangerous place. The enemies vanquished in World War I had returned. Nations were again amassing armies and navies. The winds of war were gathering. The storm that was about to erupt would be felt in every corner of the world, including mine.

Back in Uniform

THE WAR NOBODY WANTED, but everybody knew was coming, arrived on the quiet Sunday of December 7, 1941. The Japanese attack on Pearl Harbor inflicted scandalous damage on the Pacific Fleet.

At the time, details on the extent of the damage and loss of life were kept from the American people. The government did not want the world to know that much of our capability to defend the west coast of the United States was sitting at the bottom of Pearl Harbor.

On the tenth of December, I wrote a letter to the Navy Department, asking to be recalled to duty. I was sure that men who had spent any time at Annapolis would be in demand now that the country was gearing up for war. Although it arrived as a result of a tragic event, my chance to get back into uniform was at hand.

The reply from the Navy Department was not what I had expected. Instead of orders telling me where to report for duty, I received an officially worded "thanks, but no thanks" letter. The Navy did not want me.

I did not just find it puzzling, I found it bizarre. Had I offended someone at the Navy Department? After some investigative work, I discovered that in 1936, the Commerce Department had placed my name on a list of people who were of "strategic importance" in the case of a national emergency. The U.S. Government said that, at a time of war, George I. Purdy was vital to the well-being of the copper industry.

I was shocked, in an ego-boosting sort of way. I never knew that my job at Phelps-Dodge was so important, or that my job was so secure. Phelps-Dodge had been good to me. They gave me a chance at a time when jobs were scarce—a chance that I was able to turn into a career. I liked my job, but I was not going to remain land-locked during a war. Besides, Phelps-Dodge could easily produce copper without me. I was flattered but, frankly, not that invaluable.

I wrote a letter to the company's senior management, formally asking for a release from my position so that I could return to active duty. At first, they told me I was too valuable to the company's operations, especially during a war. They denied my request. However, they should have known from previous experience that I would not take "no" for an answer.

Getting back to sea was not going to be easy. I traveled to New Orleans three times to visit the district Naval office and press my case for reinstatement. They subjected me to a battery of physical examinations and interviews that seemed a waste of time given the national emergency. I felt that they were stalling—looking for something wrong with me so the Navy would not have to start a turf war with the Commerce Department.

After pressing the bosses at Phelps-Dodge, they finally gave me a formal, written release from my job. I mailed it to the Navy that very same day. Then, the weeks of waiting began as the war raged overseas.

On the morning of August 1, 1942, I arrived at my office after taking my usual stroll around the plant. With her usual efficiency, my secretary had my mail stacked on my desk. Letters of the most importance were always on the top.

She knew my plans, and how much I wanted to return to sea. That morning, a large, brown envelope was on top of the stack. The return address was the Department of the Navy, Office of Personnel, Washington, DC. I knew Uncle Sam's answer when I saw the name on the envelope:

Purdy, George I., Lt. JG USNR

That was all I needed to know. After more than a decade of being beached, I was heading back to sea.

The envelope contained my orders and my commission as a Lieutenant Junior Grade—a pleasant surprise since I had only expected to be an ensign. It probably had something to do with my age, but I liked to think that my persuasiveness had impressed them.

My orders were to report immediately to an indoctrination school at Treasure Island Naval Base, San Francisco. There were no other details; I was to pack up and leave.

Within a week, I had set out for San Francisco, with my wife and young son soon to follow. Although I was happy to be back in the Navy, I was a little apprehensive of leaving Texas and my comfortable, secure job behind. I was not the same man I was when I left the Navy. I was older and, I liked to think, wiser than the day I left Annapolis. The future was far from certain, and I had some personal concerns as to whether or not I was doing the right thing. Crazy as it may sound, I had just put my comfortable life in El Paso behind me and headed for the coast. There was no looking back.

It took a few days to drive to San Francisco. During the thirties, the United States had been a sleepy place, but the war had resuscitated it. I was amazed at this change. Every town was bustling with activity, like no other time that I had witnessed. Everyone I met had a sense of purpose. In or out of uniform, everyone was on a mission. It was reassuring, and confirmed that the decision I had made was the right one.

When I arrived at Treasure Island, the first thing I did was report in. After the usual formalities and details of settling into life on a military base, they put me into a class of forty people. The school's main purpose was to bring our long-dormant Naval training up to date.

What a change. Admittedly, civilian life had softened both me and my nautical knowledge, but I was coming up to speed faster than most. After several weeks in the classroom, the big day arrived. I was notified that I was to receive my first assignment.

At last! After battling bureaucrats and corporate bosses, red tape and run-arounds, I had made it. I was heading back to sea.

For days, speculation as to where I would be sent filled my mind. Would they assign me to a battleship, a destroyer, or a carrier? Would I be sent to the green Atlantic or to the blue Pacific?

One morning, the orders finally came down. He told me it was a very important job that was absolutely critical for Naval operations. My commanding officer instructed me to . . . head up a welding school!

I would be the "dean" of Treasure Island's welding school.

Another adventure, but not the type I had had in mind.

Treasure Island

SEAGOING VESSELS HAVE CHANGED a lot since cave dwellers built the first canoes and rafts. Over the centuries, they have become increasingly complicated devices. Likewise, all types of craftsmen, trained in a variety of skills, have been created just to build and maintain modern ships.

In the latter half of the 1800s, a new set of craftsmen was required to build ships out of metal, iron and then steel. Among them, and one of the most important, is the welder.

Naval ships suffer much wear and tear—especially at wartime when the other side is trying to blow you out of the water. Ships with holes and cracks in them have a hard time staying afloat.

As luck would have it, I was the only one in my indoctrination class who had had any industrial experience. Although I had never been a welder, the other men had spent their careers as business executives or office workers. People who knew how to work machinery, and how to manage machinery people, were in short supply.

After learning the reason for the job, and the Navy's urgent need of welders, my disappointment turned into enthusiasm. I threw everything into my mission. Every shot-up ship in the Navy depended on me.

There was one small problem: Treasure Island did not have a welding school. I had to create one from scratch. They told me to spare no expense, just get it done—yesterday, if not sooner.

First, I had to find somebody who really knew welding. With my background in metals, I had an idea of what it was and how it worked. However, I needed experts who really knew the trade.

I found a company in San Francisco that manufactured industrial welding equipment. I paid Victor Equipment Company a visit and told them my predicament. Just like the rest of the United States, they were working together to wage war. They not only supplied all the equipment I needed, but they went out of their way to help me. Their top engineers helped me design my school and they advised me on how to set up the curriculum.

I had no problem getting materials. Everything I asked for was delivered promptly. Tragic as war is, it is wonderful for getting things accomplished. I would submit a requisition and things would appear as if by magic—often overnight.

Next, I needed teachers. Luck was with me here as well. There was a massive number of recruits being processed on Treasure Island. Everyone who had any welding experience was immediately assigned to my school. Men who had, until recently, been foundry workers and garage mechanics suddenly found themselves as teachers at what was quickly becoming one of the largest welding schools in our corner of the world.

After the school was up and running, I was told to add underwater welding to the curriculum. Towing a ship into dry dock when something goes wrong below the waterline is a luxury during wartime. Many ships carried their own welders, and the bigger vessels had welders with diving experience.

Underwater diving in the first half of the twentieth century was nothing like during the latter half. Diving suits were in vogue, the kind that today can be found only in a fish aquarium or on display in a seafood restaurant. Back then, suits consisted of heavy canvas with a brass helmet and two hoses, one for a telephone-like communication system, the other for air.

The traditional diving suit was very heavy, weighing about 200 pounds. To be a diver, one had to be in excellent physical shape. Wearing the suit and engaging in underwater activity was really draining. After diving, a man would be so exhausted that he would spread out like a jellyfish when he got topside.

All the welders had to become divers, myself included. Teaching men to dive required a diving tank like the kind used in submarine rescue training. I submitted a request for one and, like everything else, the diving tank arrived within days.

Four men who had worked on salvaging a French ship that had caught fire in New York Harbor were transferred to the Treasure Island facility to serve as instructors. After we had everything set up, the fun began.

Working underwater in a big, bulky suit makes one feel like an astronaut in space. Tasks like welding, or turning bolts, are some of the most difficult that I have ever confronted.

Working underwater also provides a shocking look at life beneath the waves, where people do not usually swim. Shortly after I became a Class 2 diver, there was an accident at a San Francisco pier. We were requested to retrieve a supply of torpedo parts that had fallen into the water while being loaded aboard a ship. It was my first job as a diver, and I was shocked to find more than six feet of mud on the bottom of San Francisco Bay, mixed with all sorts of garbage and junk. It was worse than revolting.

After a year on Treasure Island, I was chafing at the bit to get to sea. I put in the request for a transfer, but was told that I was too valuable for them to send me elsewhere. However, after some persuasion, my commanding officer finally accepted my request. I was sent to Miami to undergo training for destroyer and escort duty. Leaving my family in San Francisco, I headed to Florida.

Before the war, only rich people could afford to go to Miami Beach. In the thirties, movie stars, socialites and other celebrities frequented the many hotels overlooking the Caribbean. However, after Pearl Harbor, the Navy usurped nearly all of the area's resort facilities. It was a sad loss for the rich and famous but, if you were a sailor, it was fantastic.

I was to be trained to serve as a damage control officer. The course was easy, given my experience at Annapolis. Instructors of all kinds were in short supply, and I was pressed into duty as a celestial navigation instructor. Both learning and teaching kept me very busy. There was little time for the sand and surf.

Finally, in early December of 1943, they ordered me to report for duty aboard the U.S.S. Evarts (DE-5), a destroyer escort, at the Brooklyn Navy Yard in New York. The call of the sea was finally being answered.

It was hard to leave the balmy weather of Florida for the ice and snow of the Northeast, but the excitement of being an officer on a ship kept me warm. When I arrived in New York, I was told that my ship was at target practice and I was to stay at the Commodore Hotel, another first-class establishment taken over by the Navy, until it returned.

If one has ever seen in the movies how civilians treated military personnel during World War II, it is all true. Parties, dances, free drinks, and, more importantly, respect, were experienced everywhere. We were America's defenders, out to save the world from the Triple Axis powers. Every man who wore a uniform was a hero, even if he had not been in action. I had a wonderful time in the Big Apple. It was, until that time, one of the most exciting weeks of my life.

I received word that the Evarts was not returning to New York, but would be going back to Norfolk, Virginia. I was to report on board there. The party was over. I packed up my gear and took a train to Virginia.

Virginia is a very cold place in winter, but Norfolk Naval Base had a particularly foreboding chill to it. A war can do that to a place. My new ship, the Evarts, cast an ominous shadow on the dock as I walked up to it that late afternoon, Christmas Eve. Coming aboard was, in a word, creepy. The sunshine of Miami and the excitement of New York were quickly fading memories.

In keeping with the Navy tradition, I reported right away to the captain. He was a tired-looking man, constantly smoking. This man seemed younger than me in years, but with many more miles behind him—miles he would like to forget.

"Lt. JG George I. Purdy reporting for duty, sir! I am your new damage control officer."

He gave me a cold, uncaring look. I was nothing more than a prop to him.

"Damage control officer? Already have one. You're the new gunnery officer. We're getting underway soon. Get your gear stowed. Dismissed."

I returned his salute and was escorted to my quarters, trying to hide my fear.

gunnery officer? I was to be the ship's gunnery officer? I did not even know what a gunnery officer did on a destroyer escort—the ship about to head into battle against the forces of Nazi Germany? We were going to tangle with Adolf Hitler's Wolf Packs and I was responsible for firing back. I did not know which weapons they had on board, let alone how to operate them. What sort of mess had I gotten myself into?

Welcome back to sea, George...welcome to the war...and Merry Christmas.

The Green Monster

BE CAREFUL WHAT YOU WISH FOR, you may get it.

Nothing could have been more true that long, cold Christmas night. The holiday season was going to be a nightmare.

That first night aboard, the captain had assigned me the midnight watch. While standing on the bridge, I was shocked to discover that after all of my training and all of my studies, I felt unprepared. I remembered the peacetime Navy when everything fit so neatly into place. Nothing was left undone or overlooked. There was plenty of time for a newly assigned officer or seaman to train in his new position aboard his new ship. Paperwork would be filled out, sent to a distant office where the appropriate stamps and signatures would be applied, and then sent back to the origin. Neat and snappy, the way military things were supposed to operate.

War has never been neat. It is a fluid situation that calls for change at a moment's notice, and that often means ignoring the unimportant or trivial. None of the other men aboard the Evarts seemed to know, let alone care about, my predicament. As we headed into the Atlantic, they walked through the passageways and along the deck with an air of a serious, sad purpose. There was little unnecessary talking among them. Each had his job to do and knew what was expected. They were automatic, like machines. Although most of them were still very young, their faces seemed a decade or two ahead of their bodies.

Settling into my new home wasn't easy. The last time I was at sea, I had been a teenager and the world had been at peace. Now, I was sailing into a war created by the most evil of men and ideas. Up until then, the ocean had represented freedom and life. As our ship churned through the waves towards Europe, the sea revealed its darker side. For the first time, I saw it as a place of doom, something to be feared and dreaded. Unlike the friendly, deep-blue Pacific of my youth, the Atlantic Ocean was a throbbing green monster that longed to be the means of one's death—a creature that could drown a man's soul as easily as his flesh.

Winter in the mid-Atlantic is colder than anyone could ever imagine. Even in moderate winds, the chill goes down to the marrow in your bones. It's a numbing feeling, not unlike the cold steel of a dagger being slowly driven into your body. The constant fear slowly growing inside of me kept me warmer and more alert than anything else ever could.

Well, here I was. I had given up a very comfortable and high-paying job as a civilian and then a very safe job with the Navy on Treasure Island. However, "given up" wasn't the proper term to describe my actions; I had *fought* to throw off the warm blanket of safety and security and to get into the middle of a war. I had left behind a wife and young son so that I could live aboard a freezing cold ship admidst an ocean filled with German U-boats bent on killing me and my kind. While in my earlier jobs I had been appreciated and treated well, now I was just the greenhorn gunnery officer on a ship that could be blown out of the water at any moment. If I made a mistake in my new job, people would die—myself probably among them. When the reality of the situation hit me, it made my body shiver in a way that had nothing to do with the icy wind blowing through my bones.

I quickly learned the routine of convoy duty. The Evarts and several other warships were escorting about one hundred merchant vessels to Europe. Our mission was simple: get as many of them there as possible. We used a very complex system of "zigging and zagging" to throw off any submarines following us. By changing direction at irregular times, we would make a U-boat have a difficult time aiming its torpedoes. Without the use of a radio, it took a lot of planning and mathematics to get so many ships to move at the same time, and only met with limited success.

We expected attacks from German submarines. They always attacked convoys as large as the one we were guarding. In the cold, calculated planning of war, we hoped that only the less valuable ships on the outer edge of the armada would be sent to the bottom. No one talked of the men who would die. All that mattered were the ships.

The vessels were in a constant state of readiness. The tension never ceased and the guard was never let down. Aboard the ships, all one did was sleep, eat, and perform one's assigned job. It was not the Navy that I had remembered, nor the career that I had imagined. World War II was not the old-style, gentleman's conflict that we used to read about at Annapolis. I was faced with the horrible reality of what historians were later to call "total war." All of the major nations were resigned to the exhaustive reality of a long, bloody fight. Untold misery would be the only true survivor.

Even during the daytime it was dark. The clouds were almost always with us, making the gray-green atmosphere surrounding our convoy all the more sinister and loathsome. Against all human nature, we feared both the daytime and the night. We were an easier target with the sun shining down on us, but we could also see the wake of an approaching torpedo, often with enough time to maneuver out of the way. Dusk, the time of day when most of God's creatures would be going to sleep, was the most dreaded and feared time for those on convoy duty.

I do not remember the exact day, most days were more or less the same; perhaps it was New Year's Eve. We were about midway across the Atlantic when they struck. The Wolf Packs, groups of German submarines that went after our merchant ships the way wolves would sheep, emerged from the murky depths and began to feed.

They usually picked their targets during the daytime and then waited for the cover of darkness to attack. They avoided warships like the Evarts. Not just because we could fight back, but because their mission was to stop the supply of food and materiel flowing to Europe. Their attack was silent and seemingly random. I sometimes thought of those stationed below deck who witnessed the torpedo entering the hull of the ship. What horror they must have experienced in that split second before the warhead detonated. Did time freeze for them as their eyes looked upon the steel fish that was about

50

to explode? Did they realize what it was? Did they realize that their lives were over, that they were already dead? No one will ever know. At least their end was quick. Others above deck were not so lucky.

Ahead in the distance, I heard an explosion. It was a sound not unlike rolling thunder in the mountains. A torpedo had hit and a ship was dying, along with the men she carried. It had begun. Everyone's alert level increased a notch, but not to the extent one would expect. Losing a ship or two was expected. It was just another statistic, nothing with which to be concerned.

Not too long after, I heard the cries for help as we zigzagged through the darkness. It was hard to make out, but "help" and "over here" could sometimes be heard. Others heard curses, prayers and, occasionally, the word "mother" coming out of the gloom.

The cries of the survivors fell upon sympathetic but deaf ears. None of the ships could afford to stop. We couldn't slow down to pick them up or we would become a target ourselves. If anything, we had to increase our speed to escape from harm. The men who were pleading with us to save their lives were already dead. Even if they were in lifeboats, and had a supply of food and water, they were already dead; they knew it as well as we did. Yet, they continued their increasingly desperate, shrill cries for assistance. Although we could only hear them for a few minutes, their cries of agony seemed to last for hours. Like demons cursing our souls, they called out into the darkness, eventually drowned out by the hum of the engine and the surf in our wake.

The worst place to witness the pleading of the damned was near the rear of the convoy. After an attack, one could see men in lifeboats or clinging to debris, quickly being passed by. If it was daytime or if there was enough moonlight, one could see them waving. Sometimes their faces could be made out as well. Their cries for salvation were the most desperate at the rear. They knew we were their last chance. We knew it too. We also knew that nothing would be done to save them. As they faded out of sight, to slowly die in the middle of the heartless ocean, they ceased being lives and became statistics. Perhaps a name on a memorial would mark their passing, but that would be all. They were just another drop in the sea of misery that the world had plunged itself into.

In the days it took to cross the Atlantic, the horror we felt was not from the casualties we had witnessed but from the fact that any of us could have been among the poor souls whose lives would end at sea. We had only seen a single convoy; there were hundreds of them during the war. So many ships went down at the hands of the Wolf Packs that the authorities didn't even bother with the actual number. They just calculated the total tonnage lost per month. Only a few ships were sunk in my first convoy. It was considered a success.

While assigned to the Evarts, I performed only two round trips across the Atlantic guarding convoys, but it was more than enough for a dozen lifetimes. After the experience, I discovered that my apprehension of my ability to be the gunnery officer was unfounded. The instinct from all my training took control and, during a rare idle moment, the captain told me I had done an excellent job.

His words were appreciated, but not comforting. For me, the romance of war, the spell under which almost all young men at the time fell, had disappeared. True, I felt it was my place to defend my country from the enemies that threatened its existence. In spite of my earlier concerns over the path I had chosen, I felt that it was the right one. However, after my first time of staring into the face of my own mortality, it became nothing more than a job—a dirty job that needed to be completed as soon as possible. In the middle of the Atlantic I learned that the adventure of the ocean had been replaced with the horror that is a world at war. The most dangerous creature on or in the ocean had become man.

After reaching Europe, our next destination was the Mediterranean— the ancient ocean that was once the domain of the Egyptians, Romans and Greeks. As a boy, I had read of the countless sea battles that had been fought there since the human race became "civilized." Alexander, Julius Caesar, and Napoleon all fought battles in its warm, blue waters. Now, the folly of man had turned it into a battleground yet again.

Only, on this page of its history, I would be a part of it.

The Pillars of Hercules

THE CIRCUMSTANCES SURROUNDING my first days as a foreign tourist could have been a lot better, but at least I was beginning to see the world—even though it was in the process of tearing itself apart.

Our next destination was the coast of North Africa, one of the few places American soldiers had begun to fight Hitler's armies. Within hours of our arrival at the port of Casablanca, the crew was told that three German submarines were heading down the coast of Portugal towards Gibraltar, with the obvious aim of getting into the Mediterranean. The Evarts was to be one of seven warships sent to "greet them."

We arrived at dusk. Although I was busy with the task of getting ready to hunt submarines, I took a few moments to watch the sun set over the Atlantic. It was the first time since setting sail from Norfolk that I had seen something beautiful. I thought of the stories of the ancient Greek heroes that I had learned in school. I remembered that the former name of the straits was the Pillars of Hercules, named after Zeus' son, the hero of classical times.

It also came to mind that the "pillars" marked the entrance into Hades, the abode of the dead, otherwise known as Hell—a place that seemed not unlike what the Atlantic had become. I returned my attention to the task at hand.

All ships were set for ASW, Anti-Submarine Warfare. The Evarts was on an even higher state of alert because the convoy's commodore was on board. We all wanted to look our best for him. In spite of the less formal environment of a ship at wartime, the boss was always someone you wanted to impress in any business.

During the middle of the night, the sonar operators detected an underwater object that appeared to be a sub. We began tracking it. The game was afoot.

The technology of the time was unlike anything that the militaries of the world would later develop. Sonar, the ability to find objects underwater by using sound, was far from reliable. Due to the war, the technology had been developed in a hurry. It was not uncommon to send factory technicians aboard ships during all but the most hazardous of missions.

Where the machine failed, the man became indispensable. Good sonar operators were invaluable to crew members. After all, if one could tell the difference between an enemy submarine and a school of fish over all the static and other background noise of a WWII-era sonar system, it could mean the difference between dying young or living to be an old man with grandchildren. The technicians earned their pay.

Just because something was big and underwater didn't necessarily mean that it would kill you. To sonar, porpoises look a lot like submarines. It was probably Mother Nature's cruelest joke during the Second World War. These rather playful, peaceful creatures have the rather annoying habit of staying on course and traveling at the exact same speed as a German U-boat. Sometimes hundreds of them would be swimming in formation and a sonar operator would mistake them for the enemy below.

Spotting such a target, later termed a "biological" by the Navy, would often bring a warship to general quarters. Quite a few warships were destroyed because someone mistook a submarine for those gentle creatures of the deep.

Close to dawn, we felt we had a contact with a hard target so we began our attack with depth charges. All of the ships in our little armada went after that one sub. The tactics of the time were clumsy and crude compared to the fire-and-forget methods of later decades. The idea was to drop enough depth charges so that we were bound to hit it. It was several hours of rolling the charges off the stern of the ships, and watching the explosions shoot out of the water in the wake of our ship—an especially eerie spectacle during a full moon.

54

It was a hair-raising night. Seven ships were running around the perilously narrow Straits of Gibraltar trying to avoid hitting each other, avoid getting hit by enemy torpedoes, and find three German submarines among hundreds of porpoises that looked a lot like submarines. Everyone was trying to avoid getting hit by everybody else. God only knows what the porpoises thought. It would have been a great plot for an ancient Greek comedy, if they had had U-boats and depth charges.

As the sun rose in the sky, one of our lookouts spotted an oil slick and what appeared to be a life jacket floating on the surface of the water. German sub captains would often release oil and shoot "debris" out of torpedo tubes, in the attempt to trick the pursuing ship into thinking that they had been sunk. It was a tactic that several Hollywood movies would later make immortal. We saw no other indication of submarines, either above or below the water's surface. We thought we had gotten him, but we weren't positive. The sinking was described as a "probable."

Not all the dangers of the Mediterranean came from German submarines. Some came from people with whom we were not supposed to be at war. While it was generally believed that Spain was neutral during World War II, many Spaniards weren't. Being a fascist country under the iron rule of Francisco Franco, the country had many pro-Nazi elements. They did not want to see us win. Many lived on the coast near Gibraltar, and the Spanish government didn't care what they did.

The night after our attack on the subs, we were tied up at a quay for the onboard clean-up that was routine after a battle. Suddenly, there was a deafening roar. The ship anchored next to us was rocked by a massive explosion. The concussion was so powerful that our ship began to rock as if it were in a storm. Everyone aboard the Evarts jumped to their battle stations. The first thought that came into my head was that one of the subs had escaped and was now coming after us. We were tied up in a row like sitting ducks. A few torpedoes could have sent our entire convoy to the bottom.

It was not a submarine. A German-built delayed-action mine

had sunk the ship next to us. It was most likely planted by a Spanish diver who had swum out from shore; it may have been a German diver who was "on vacation" in Spain. It's amazing what "tourists" will bring with them when they visit the beach.

Whoever it was, they knew where to plant the mine in order to inflict as much damage as possible. The destroyer sank in a few minutes. I never did learn the casualty figure. Spain succeeded in staying out of the war. The nation's fascist dictator, Francisco Franco, stayed in power until his death from old age in 1975.

Our patrol of the area continued for a while. There were a few other attacks on what we thought were submarines. However, there was never any conclusive evidence of our success. Our ship was once attacked by German dive bombers, but the Evarts suffered no damage in the incident.

Compared to others, the time that I spent hunting for submarines in the Mediterranean was relatively peaceful. It certainly beat crossing the Atlantic. It was one of the few times during the war that I would be able to relax.

Eventually, the Evarts was sent back to the Atlantic, through the Pillars of Hercules and into the dark Hades that the ocean had become. I dreaded being on convoy duty for the rest of the war.

Fortunately, it was not to be. I did not know it at the time, but as we left the ancient waters of the Mediterranean, something was happening inside the complicated workings of the Navy Department. Somebody said something to somebody, or reported something in a report, or noticed something in a notice. Anyway, the "why" never did matter to me—the results did.

As I rode shotgun on my last convoy of ships across the Atlantic, workers were swarming over a large steel mass outside of Boston. Riveters, engineers, steelworkers, and all sorts of other talented men had gathered to build a wonderful structure that was to be one of the most important classrooms of my life: a ship.

It never bothered me that it was only one of hundreds that the assembled workers were constructing. They were building *my* ship. The Navy was giving me my own command.

George Irwin Purdy at
about eighteen months.

Keeping cool with friends and a garden hose,
just after the First World War.

My first plane ride, sometime after the First World War. That's me in the rear cockpit.

George Purdy, age fourteen.

George Edgar Purdy in his late years.

The Destroyer Escort U.S.S. *Evarts*

credit: Author's Collection

My first year at Annapolis.
It was the "Age of the Gentleman."

My team at Treasure Island in front of the diving tank we used to train men in underwater welding techniques.

Graduates of the welding school from the U.S.S. *Tiburon*. August 14, 1943.

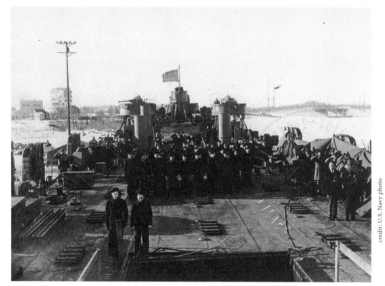

The commissioning ceremony of the LST-973. Boston, 1945.

Breaking all the rules: the ship that wasn't supposed to be christened, is. The christening of the LST-973 on December 27, 1944.

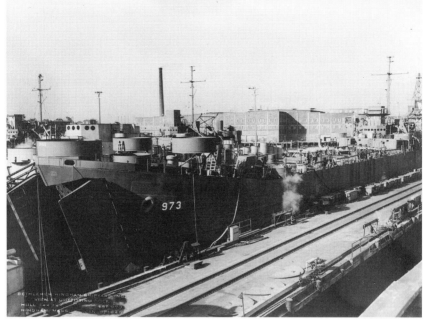

The LST-973 under construction in Boston.

Skipper

FOR SOMEONE WHO GREW UP in temperate climates, I wondered how the inhabitants of the northeastern corner of the United States could function in wintertime. Boston was cold during the 1944 holiday season. Still, like Christmas always is, it was a joyous occasion.

After the Evarts returned to Norfolk from its second run across the Atlantic, I checked into the base hospital with a very bad case of seasickness. It was an affliction that would hit me on and off and was interfering with my duties. Although I still wanted to be at sea, the captain thought it would be a good idea to transfer me to shore duty for a while, in hopes that I would get over it.

No matter how much one loves the sea or life aboard a ship, the human body was still designed for land. Sailors of all ages and with all levels of experience can come down with seasickness, much like mountain climbers can get altitude sickness—it just hits you when it does. It was not something to be embarrassed about, but a challenge to be overcome.

After my tour with the Evarts, I was assigned to the Amphibious Training Center in Norfolk, where I was to be instructed in the command functions of the smaller support ships, among them LSTs.

The term LST is an acronym for Landing Ship Tank. It was a fair-sized, multipurpose cargo ship designed to work anywhere. LSTs had flat bottoms and front doors that could beach on a shoreline. The doors would open and troops, tanks, and jeeps could drive off. An LST could also operate as a conventional cargo ship.

During my training at Norfolk, it became apparent that they planned to assign me to an LST. I had no idea what my position

64

aboard would be. It seemed like they were preparing me to do everything.

One day after class, my commanding officer stopped by to see me. "Lieutenant?"

"Yes, sir!" I replied.

"There is a ship currently being constructed up in Boston, at the Bethlehem-Hingham shipyard. An LST, number 973. You'll be her skipper. Get up there as soon as you receive your formal orders."

"Aye, aye sir!" I replied with military instinct.

There was no fanfare; just a simple assignment as far as he was concerned. To me, it was a lifetime accomplishment and an honor that, only a few years ago, had been beyond my imagination. If I had been carrying any books, I probably would have dropped them like a giddy schoolgirl.

Then it hit me: responsibility. Not that I didn't know what responsibility meant, but I would be responsible for the safety and welfare of an entire ship and crew during wartime. I was happy, but the cold reality of the task that lay ahead was sobering.

A few days after my schooling was finished, I found myself on the outskirts of Boston, Massachusetts in a massive shipyard, my next adventure awaiting me.

I reported to the yard captain and handed him my orders. In spite of his many responsibilities, he was a jovial fellow who seemed to enjoy delivering ships to their new owners. There was probably some concern in his job, too. Not unlike a car salesman handing the keys of a sports car to a teenager, one hopes he isn't heading off to his death.

"LST-973. . .here it is. Yeah, she slips into the water tomorrow night at about 2100."

Great, I thought. Then I asked him about the christening ceremony.

A strange look appeared on his face. "We're pretty busy here, Lieutenant. Only have time to christen one in ten." LSTs didn't warrant the fanfare that the bigger ships enjoyed.

Well, that wasn't acceptable. Superstition dies hard. My ship was going to have a proper christening and anything less would be blasphemous. I thanked the yard captain and told him I'd be back the following night.

In order to give a ship a proper christening one needs two things: a bottle of good champagne and a woman to smash the bottle on the side of the ship's hull. Champagne was easy to find in Boston, but a woman, well. . .

I knew nobody in Boston, male or female. At first, the problem seemed insurmountable. Where does one find an appropriate lady for a ship christening a couple of days after Christmas during a war?

Back then, women who were in the Navy were called WAVEs. In the days before women at Annapolis became a common site, they served in a support role. Out of the blue, I telephoned the local WAVE headquarters. I planned to ask the first officer to whom I spoke if she would do the honor. A lieutenant picked up the phone. I introduced myself and asked what I thought was a very simple question.

"Would you please come christen my ship tomorrow night?"

There was dead silence on the other end of the line. After a few moments, she responded.

"I've heard a lot of propositions in my time, but this is a first."

After a more detailed explanation, I assured her that I was very serious. She then became excited and agreed, but asked if she could bring along a friend. "No problem," I told her.

A couple of hours before the roll-off, the man who would be my navigation officer aboard the 973, George Jess, and I arrived at the Boston train station. Standing at the information desk, admidst a sea of people, were two young women in uniform, one a lieutenant, the other an ensign. A broad smile broke on both their faces as they saw us.

That night at nine o'clock, the two WAVEs, the yard captain (amazed that I was making such a big deal over the launching),

Jess, and I stood out in the cold at the side of what would soon be my new home. It had begun to snow, which added to the holiday spirit. A few of the workmen were looking at us as well, probably because we were holding up their schedule.

The lieutenant took the bottle of champagne that I had purchased earlier that evening, and called out into the night air, "I christen thee LST-973, the finest ship that will ever sail the sea." With a muffled crash, the chicken-wire-encased bottle was broken on the bow. My new command then slid into the water with all the grace of a child's toy being tossed into a bathtub. We applauded against the sound of the yard's welders and riveters who went on with their work, oblivious to what we were doing.

The next morning, the real work began, and the full impact of my situation began to settle on my shoulders. The 973 would have a crew of one hundred and twenty men of whom only four, myself included, had any experience at sea. I was to be their captain. The safety and welfare of all these men would be my responsibility.

The ship got underway for the first time, heading down to Boston's Commonwealth Pier to be outfitted. Two days later, we took her out for a trial run. It was only for a day, but long enough for our first mishap. Ice from the James River had gotten into Boston Harbor and one of our propellers got stuck. The damage wasn't bad but it did affect our speed. My orders were to get it repaired someplace else. There were other ships coming off the line and they wanted us on our way. We spent about another week amassing supplies and installing equipment, with little time to get acquainted with the ship and its crew. There was a war raging. Like a kid who had grown up, they kicked us out of Boston Harbor. We set sail for the Pacific.

Return to Paradise

THE LST-973 BEGAN ITS SERVICE in the early days of January 1945. The war was winding down in Europe. Hitler and the evil empire he had built upon a once proud and decent civilization would soon be erased from the earth. However, the war in the Pacific, against the Empire of Japan, was another matter.

There was no end in sight for the Pacific war. Japan's armies had been beaten back throughout Asia, its cities were being bombed, and its ships were being sunk. Yet there was no sign that the country would collapse. Even if the millions of soldiers still occupying vast tracts of China and the Far East could be destroyed, as it was unlikely they would ever surrender, an invasion of the Japanese archipelago was still imminent. A forested, mountainous country in most places, it would be an epic battle of Biblical death and destruction when the allied armies landed on its shores.

However, the shooting part of the war was still a long way off for me. Those first days as skipper aboard the 973 were some of the most educational of my life. I was filled with both apprehension and satisfaction knowing that I had been given a ship to command. True, it was not as "exciting" as a destroyer or a carrier; it was a support ship, small by Navy standards. But, it was my ship, my crew, my home.

We made our way to Norfolk to take on our first cargo, a load of jeeps and trucks that we were to bring with us to the Panama Canal. We made our way through the Caribbean, my first time sailing its waters, and down into Panama.

It was my first trip to Panama since I was a seaman aboard the California. We had stopped there when I was a teenager. That was before Annapolis, before my career in metals, before everything—almost twenty years earlier. Back then, the U.S. Canal Zone was a sleepy, quiet place. But, like the rest of the United States, it had been transformed into a bustling, wartime operations center. There was little time to see the sights and there were few sights to see. We unloaded our cargo, took on another one, and headed into the Pacific. From a sailor's point of view, I was home.

If the Atlantic is a big, green monster, then the Pacific is a quiet blue dove. It was with a sense of relief that we steamed out of the last lock of the canal and into the ocean of my youth. Although it was only a little more than a year ago that I had left my post at Treasure Island, it felt like a lifetime had passed since I had seen it.

We steamed up along the coast of Mexico en route to my hometown, San Diego. As we approached U.S. waters, I instructed the navigator to head for a small group of islands close to our destination. There was a circle I needed to complete.

We arrived at the Coronado Islands early in the morning. The scent of the breeze wafting from the Mexican coast told me that spring was coming. After the ship came to a stop, I went on deck and gazed out on a memory.

The island itself was the same, except for the intrusion of man. A fair-sized, but obviously abandoned, building overlooked the small cove in which Harry and I once swam.[1] The human race had discovered my little paradise, but it was still largely intact.

All of the memories and all of the good times from that summer long ago came rushing back. I imagined myself walking along the shore, sleeping on the beach, and swimming in the surf. It seemed like only yesterday that my real life was a dream and my all-too-short time on the island was reality. I've heard that you can never go home again, but I did and it was wonderful. It was a calm, bright sunny day without a cloud in the sky, just the way I remembered it.

I used the public address system, proceeding to tell the entire crew the story of my adventures on the island so many years in the past, when the world was saner and more civilized. I hadn't planned on telling my story, but it felt right to do so. I wanted to share that summer of my boyhood with the men for whose lives I was responsible.

I told my tale of tarantulas, bones of Chinese sailors, and fish that were capable of pulling two boys out to sea. Most of the crew came up on deck to take a look. Nobody said a word, perhaps because it was a peaceful moment brought on by the story of a peaceful time. It was a tale of innocence in a world that had grown evil; one of contentment and peace in a world that had none; a brief moment of sanity on a planet gone insane. They seemed to enjoy the break from routine and the chance to play tourist. It was the first time since we left Boston that the ship was really my home.

My narration on Dead Man's Island lasted about two hours, but it seemed like an entire day. After I finished, I gave the order to head off to San Diego where we were to pick up the mail. Looking back on the summer of my youth as it faded out of sight, I realized my good fortune. One gives thanks on such occasions, and I thanked the fish that almost dragged me out to sea. Everything beautiful is also dangerous, the sea being no exception. At an early age, I had learned respect for the god, Neptune. I would now carry that lesson into a war.

Dead Man's Island faded out of view and out of mind. It was back to the business of running a U.S. Navy ship.

We only stopped briefly in San Diego for mail, not even tying up to dock. A mail boat pulled up alongside us and we switched bags. Like the rest of the U.S. war machine, the harbor was a very busy place. We had used up our tourist time on the Coronados. With our bent propeller, we were ordered to Seattle to make repairs before heading across the Pacific.

As we made our way up the California coast, I remembered when my father took me aboard his merchant ship for the short trip from San Diego to San Francisco. It was my first trip on a boat, my introduction to the sea, and the beginning of a lifelong journey.

While heading up the coast, I made a ship-to-shore call to my father at his retirement home in San Francisco. The next day, he met me at the dock. The old sailor almost burst with pride when he saw me come down the gangplank. In all his years at sea, he had never made captain. His son had done better than he had, which meant he had succeeded as a father. He shook my hand and embraced me, showing more emotion than I ever remembered him expressing.

I gave him a tour of my command and introduced him to several members of the crew. Even though he was there to see his son, the officer in him was anxious to see the Navy's latest technology. I spent the next few hours explaining our gear, the way I would in a training session. He was as excited as a new recruit, but as familiar with a ship as any of us.

Another VIP visited the LST 973 while her propeller was being straightened out: Harry Holloway, who was working for Boeing, stopped by after I gave him a call and told him that I was in town.

Harry had settled in Seattle after school and we had corresponded with each other over the years. We had parted ways as boys and now we were grown men fighting a war. I commanded a ship, while he helped build airplanes.

Harry found himself in the rather awkward position of not knowing anyone aboard my ship, but them knowing him. It was only a few days since we had stopped at Dead Man's Island and I had told the tale of our youthful adventure. Harry, who always let things roll off his back, just took it all in stride.

Inviting your father aboard your ship is one thing for a captain, but bringing a boyhood friend aboard is quite another. Harry didn't let up on the jokes or wisecracks, jestfully questioning my ability to keep a ship this size from running aground. I didn't mind it at all. It was good to be on a ship with Harry again.

The only embarrassing part was how he constantly called me "Irwin," my middle name. Up until high school, everyone called me Irwin to avoid confusion with my father, also named George. I flinched every time he said it. My crew picked up on the name, but they didn't exploit this newly discovered fact. They never had the occasion to use "Irwin" over "George," since the first name of every ship captain is always "Skipper."

Harry had his fun, and I even let him take the helm when we cruised around the harbor to test our new propeller. Before we parted, we promised to keep in touch and, as it would turn out, remain best friends for the rest of our lives.

It was time to leave; there was a war waiting. The next day, as we departed for the Pacific, we passed a small rocky outcropping that was used as a navigation point. My father said he would be there to see me off.

I looked for him, but even with binoculars I could not spot him. Yet, I knew he was there because I could feel it. I stood at attention and gave a sharp and snappy salute. A torch had been passed and we both knew it.

It was a moment that every father and son experience in their lives, a reckoning and understanding that can never be properly put into words. At the time, I thought it was rather amazing that a piece of stray ice in Boston Harbor could lead me back to the place where I had fallen in love with the sea, as well as to the two men who had had the greatest influence on my life. Fate exists, but it must be exploited and used, not left to stand still and happen on its own.

We were heading into a war. Fate and I would once again be crossing paths.

The Wild West

HAWAII WAS NOT WHAT I HAD EXPECTED. Just as it is today, it was a tourist attraction; a beautiful place—perhaps too beautiful for its own good.

Before the war, only those with money could afford to go to Hawaii. Most people on the mainland knew very little about the remote U.S. territory in the middle of the Pacific. However, during the war, millions of men stopped on the island on their way to battle. Many were overwhelmed by its majesty and beauty, and they returned after the war to develop its tourist industry. I'm fortunate to have seen it before that happened.

There were sailors and soldiers everywhere. A multitude had taken over the island, as well as the resort hotels along Waikiki. For my ship and crew, it was our last taste of the U.S. before heading into the unknown. There was not much to do except go for a swim or lie on the beach. I saw many guys on surfboards, and decided to give it a try.

On the beach, there was a shriveled-looking old lady renting boards. A deposit was required in addition to the rental charge. When I asked for a receipt, and told her my name, she looked up in astonishment. Her last name was Purdy, too. We talked for awhile about our respective families' histories, but could not find a connection.

Yet, it was probably some sort of sign. I fell in love with the sport and would continue surfing long after most men had gone to retirement homes.

After our few days in paradise, we headed for Guam and then for the Philippines—out of the area deemed safe and into the war zone.

It took us little more than a week to make our way to San Pedro Bay, Philippines. I'll never forget it. It was the greatest sight I have ever seen. The armada that had been assembled there was like nothing I could have ever imfsagined. The harbor was filled with ships of all kinds: carriers, battleships, cruisers, destroyers. For a moment, I wondered if it was our entire fleet at anchor.

We were assigned to an anchorage in the northern part of the bay. Crowded as it was, there was still room for us.

Shortly after we secured sea-detail, the officer of the deck came running down to my quarters waving a piece of paper. "Captain! Look at this! Look what our signalman just received."

The message was from a British ship anchored about five hundred yards in front of us. It read:

"Our first mate will be floating by; if you want him, you can have him."

It was a strange message and I wondered if it was a joke. After all, the British were known for their dry, tongue-in-cheek sense of humor. I went on deck and looked overboard. Sure enough, the face-down body of a man in shorts was floating by our ship. He was obviously dead.

It was a strange situation in which to find oneself. Should I leave the body in the water or fish him out? The British navy, whose practices were alien to me, didn't seem to want him. For all we knew, he might have been executed. At that point, there was little we could do to help the man.

I thought about it for a few minutes and decided to let someone else recover the body and fill out the paperwork. We were carrying a cargo of aircraft engines and spare parts destined for the northern part of the island where the Marines were fighting the Japanese. I was receiving daily messages to deliver my cargo as soon as possible. We were to leave early the next day, and thus had very little time.

After all, we were new to the neighborhood.[2] It was a different navy and the dead body was none of our business. We headed out the next morning and delivered our cargo.

During a war, things have a way of getting lost. After all, there is a lot of stuff to keep track of. Militaries don't just operate on bullets and guns. If you can destroy the enemy's supply of shoes, you can literally bring him to his knees.

Captains are responsible for everything aboard their ships—everything. Failure to pay attention to this fact can lead to a career-threatening, or embarrassing situation.

While moving supplies through the Philippines, we often had to use unconventional port facilities, like a sandy beach. LSTs were designed for this unconventionality and unpredictability. A captain of an LST was supposed to be an expert on near-shore conditions, so that his ship would never get damaged.

En route to one destination, we stopped briefly at an inlet near the port of Zamboanga. When I gave the order to weigh anchor, a rather embarrassing problem ensued.

The anchor wouldn't budge. It had gotten stuck on a coral reef and showed no sign of coming loose. We tried everything from moving the ship to wiggling the anchor chain, but nothing would budge it. Finally, we tried to pull it out by brute force. I ordered everyone away from the bow of the ship, and then turned on the winch.

The whole ship creaked as its stern slowly rose out of the water. The weight on the anchor must have been enormous. It stayed put, but the chain didn't.

What sounded like an explosion reverberated through the 973. The massive steel chain had broken and our anchor was a permanent addition to a coral reef.

At least we were free. There was no damage to the ship itself, but we no longer had an anchor. I knew that we had to keep our busy schedule. There was also the question of responsibility. Although I had a clear conscience, and had tried everything imaginable to free us, the United States Navy was still short an anchor and I had decided where to stop. I knew that I might have to pay for it.

The incident resulted in the ordering of my only "commando"

operation of the war. Up the coast, there was a Naval supply depot that had everything a ship needed, including anchors—anchors just the right size for an LST.

We approached under the cover of darkness and we beached, just like dozens of LSTs do every day. If we acted like we knew what we were doing, nobody would ask any questions. For obvious reasons, they kept the anchors close to the waterline.

Several of my men went ashore and attached a winch cable to one of the anchors. We pulled it in quickly and attached it to the broken chain. We were in and out in about an hour. The only one who noticed was probably some poor clerk who had to explain to his commanding officer how he lost an anchor weighing thousands of pounds. Too bad, but all's fair in love and war.[3]

After our tour in the Philippines, we received orders to head north to a place we had all heard about: Okinawa, the site of a two-month-long battle that had turned into one of the bloodiest battles in which U.S. forces had ever been engaged. The island's bases would be the staging area for an all-out assault on Japan.[4] Our ship would probably make several trips between Okinawa and the supply depots in the Philippines. It would only be a matter of time before my crew and I would find ourselves supporting a beach assault, probably Kyushu. After all, LSTs were designed to be invasion support ships.

Given their slow speed, about ten knots at the most, we used to joke that "LST" meant "Long, Slow Target." The closer we got to the enemy, the less of a joke it became. While traveling across the Pacific, we had heard that Germany had been defeated and Hitler was dead, but the Allies were still peeling away the Japanese Empire. The inner core remained intact. It would be at least another two years before the war would be over.

But far away, in the New Mexico desert, the military had successfully tested something that would change all that. Very soon, two cities in Japan would be reduced to ashes as the violent age of the atom was ushered in.

Brave New World

OKINAWA WAS A BATTLEFIELD like no other. Guns were firing, bullets were flying in all different directions, and people were screaming at the top of their lungs. Fires were springing up everywhere, terror reigned in the streets, and the injured were strewn about like rag dolls. All was chaos. Order was impossible. If there was ever a place of pure madness, this was it.

Oddly, the war was over and the Japanese army was nowhere to be seen.

When the Japanese surrender was announced on August 15, 1945, everyone was surprised, relieved and elated. Although we had heard President Truman's announcement that a new and powerful weapon had been dropped on two Japanese cities, we didn't think it would make much of a difference. We were wrong.

Many of the soldiers and sailors on Okinawa had lived through the horror of the battle and were not looking forward to the next one, which would probably be much worse. The war had been raging for almost four years and everyone was tired of it. The Emperor of Japan's announcement that his government would agree to unconditional surrender was probably met with more glee than any other news in history. Under such conditions, military men can be uncontrollable.

I hadn't lost a single man during the war and I didn't plan on losing one just after it. Guns were being fired in celebration and bullets don't discriminate.

I ordered everyone aboard ship and pulled up the boarding ladder. Nobody was to leave or come aboard. Guards were posted to make sure that nobody approached. I didn't give the order to shoot anyone who came too close, but given the right circumstances, I might have. It's funny how the highest state of alert aboard the 973 was because of other Americans.

Alcohol was, and still is, strictly forbidden aboard United States Navy ships. However, during wartime, rules are usually bent. Members of the crew were permitted to bring booze aboard the 973, but they could not consume it while on the ship. To ensure that the crew abided by this rule, I stored the alcohol in a locker to which only I had the key.

I was not going to let anyone off the ship to celebrate, so I "struck the main brace." In other words, I opened up the locker and let everyone on board have one beer or a shot of whiskey. We toasted the end of the long conflict and the fact that we had survived. The men didn't seem to mind being cooped up on the ship during such an important time. They were happy with the thought that they would soon be on their way home. A country that was still left standing awaited them.

Although the war was formally over, hostilities would not cease completely until the end of the month. Kamikaze attack planes were still around, as were Japanese submarines. Stopping two massive armies is not as easy as hitting a button on a machine. Things take time to cool down. It's at this time, when the guard is down, that men can die.

We were in Okinawa until the rioting died down. We unloaded our cargo and headed back to the Philippines, unsure as to what would come next.

Our orders were to transport a mobile hospital unit. When one of my men handed me the manifest, I was amazed at what I saw. Are they joking, I thought? So soon after the surrender?

Vessel: LST-973
Cargo: U.S. Army 71st Evacuation Hospital Unit
Destination: Yokohama

From One World to the Other

WITH 365 DAYS IN THE YEAR, a ship's log has a lot of pages. Given the length of a sea voyage, war or no war, most entries are trivial and mundane. However, one date in the log of the 973 stood out from the rest: September 12, 1945.

In relation to the other events of the time, it was twenty-five days since the Emperor of Japan had addressed his subjects and announced that the war, which had taken the lives of some fifty million people, was finally over. It was only ten days since General MacArthur had stood on the deck of the battleship Missouri, anchored in the middle of Tokyo Bay, and formally accepted the surrender from a nation that had never known defeat.

For me, it was the day that I would set foot in Japan for the very first time.

It was late morning when we first spotted the picture postcard mountain known as Fujisan—the first time anyone on board had ever seen it. As we approached the shores of our very recent enemy, you could feel the tension slowly rise throughout the ship. Most of the crew of the 973 had lost friends in the war. Some had lost relatives. Many had died in the numerous battles that had been fought: Coral Sea, Guadalcanal, Midway and a dozen other places. As it would turn out, those obscure names would go down as some of the greatest naval engagements of all time. Points on a map that would be in the history books.

But, to me, each place-name was the death of a friend, someone I had spent the early years of my life with, had shared my goals and dreams with. To this day, whenever the name of one of these places is uttered, I always remember the face of a young man who would never know the honor of growing old.

Around noon, our ship and a few other LSTs and destroyers were passing Oshima, a large island off the coast of the Izu Peninsula, south of Tokyo Bay. Without warning, there was a thunderous boom from its beaches. It was the distinct sound of a shore gun carrying over the waves. The shell hit the water several hundred yards away.

It was just one shell, but after what we experienced, it was one shell too many. Those of us who had survived the previous bloody years, had done so by not taking any chances. The captain of the destroyer that was directly astern of us ordered his ship to turn around and head towards the island. When his guns came within range, he let loose with everything he had and pulverized a small corner of the island. When the smoke cleared, the guns of Oshima were silenced forever.

It was probably just some poor, scared, trigger-happy Japanese soldier or sailor who had decided to fire on us, much to his error. It may have been the last naval engagement of the war.

We steamed into Yokohama around two in the afternoon. Surprisingly, the approaching coastline gave the observer no indication that there had ever been a war. It was, in a word, eerie. There was no indication of bombardment, or any other signs of the mass destruction for which war is famous. It was just another harbor with ships tied up along piers and sailors going to and fro.

We beached our ship on a seaplane ramp near what today is called Yokohama's North Pier. I was more careful than usual. The incident with the anchor in the Philippines was still fresh in my mind, and I had no desire to be a captain who lost his command just days after the war was over.

We didn't expect the Japanese to be very friendly so soon after the end of the war. The crews of the ships arriving in Yokohama were to be given liberty, but officers were told to wear their side arms at all times. Sailors could travel only in close proximity to their ships and they had to be in groups of three or more. We were under strict orders not to walk down any side streets or into any residential areas.

80

We beached our ship, opened our bow doors, and unloaded our passengers and cargo. With no fanfare, I came ashore to take a look around.

Japan. The Land of the Rising Sun. The nation that had terrified so much of the world, saying that it would never be defeated. Here I was, a sailor in the navy that had destroyed one of the most powerful military machines of all time.

I cannot accurately put into words the feeling I had as I stepped onto the shore. Perhaps a feeling of deep satisfaction mixed with exhaustive relief comes the closest.

Posterity and personal memories aside, we still had a job to do. After most of the work was finished at our landing site, I took a walk down the waterfront. It was late in the afternoon. As the sun started to drop low in the sky and cast shadows along the shoreline, I finally had a moment to reflect on my situation.

It was another turning point in my life, much like that rainy afternoon when my father gave me my uncle's gift. All of a sudden it hit me like a ton of bricks: the war was over. It was over, through, finished, kaput! There would be no more sad letters from faraway places and news of friends dying, no more worrying about dive bombers coming at us from out of the sun, or a kamikaze suicide attack setting us ablaze, and no more news of people being killed by the millions.

The Second World War was at an end. It was now a matter for historians to worry about, not for young men to die over.

First Contact

IT'S A UNIQUE EXPERIENCE to arrive in a foreign land with a conquering army. Taking my first walk around Japan, basically a stroll in the area surrounding my ship, was not what one would expect.

I was no longer filled with sadness or remorse. Instead, I was filled with curiosity, a sense of wonder as to what the future held in store.

I walked along the docks near the seaplane landing where we had beached the ship. There were no Japanese to be found. Curious, but not the least bit surprising.

After walking a short distance, I stopped and sat down on a concrete barrier at the edge of a canal, near what appeared to be an old, abandoned barge. I lit up a cigarette, taking in the moment and my new surroundings.

Just then, out of the corner of my eye, I saw something move on top of the old barge. I looked again and there it was: the distinct outline of the top of a man's head. Every few seconds, it would pop up and down like a jack-in-the-box. Under different circumstances, it would have been comical.

Although Yokohama Port had only recently been enemy territory, I was more curious than concerned. However, the caution was still there. The .45 on my hip made things easier.

I walked over to the barge, slowly climbed up onto the deck, and started walking up towards the hatch.

I didn't draw my side arm as I approached the open hatch and peered inside. I wanted to see who it was that had taken such an interest in my presence.

The first Japanese people that I ever met were a grizzled old barge captain and a woman who was apparently his wife. They seemed to be in their late sixties, but may have been older.

I was greeted by two people in a state of sheer terror. They were on their knees, hands covering their faces, shaking like leaves. They were probably convinced that they were about to die at the hands of a foreign monster.

At first, their behavior seemed rather irrational, but then I put myself in their place. Their whole world was gone. Perhaps they had had a son, maybe two, who had died during the war that had ended less than a month ago. Their country had been devastated, many of their neighbors had died, and their city had been set ablaze by the Americans. Now, they thought their lives were about to end at the hands of the American sailor who had invaded their home and was towering over them with a gun strapped to his side.

I didn't speak a word of their language and they didn't speak a word of mine. Nevertheless, I had to let them know that they were not in any danger from me—from any of us—before their hearts gave out.

I motioned for the old man to come up the ladder onto the deck. I didn't know it at the time, but Japanese and Americans have very different ways of signaling "come here," so it took a while for him to get the idea.

When he got up the nerve, he stood and climbed up the ladder. He was visibly trembling as he got to the top, constantly looking back at his wife, probably wondering if he would ever see her again.

When he reached the top, I motioned for him to sit across from me, which he did with all the caution and fear that a mouse would show a very large cat.

If you have ever been in a similar situation, you probably discovered that, although languages may be different, there are some tones of voice and gestures that are universal. Smiling, laughing, shouting, and crying are always expressed in the same way. So, when this poor barge captain arrived at what he probably thought would be his execution, I had to show him that I meant no harm. I did what any red-blooded American sailor in 1945 would do as a gesture of friendship: I offered him a cigarette.

He froze. He looked at the outstretched hand holding a pack of cigarettes, then at me, and then at the cigarettes again, not knowing what to make of the situation. A man who expected to be shot by a big, ugly American was instead being offered a cigarette. He now looked more puzzled than afraid. At another place and time, the scene would have been laughable

At first he refused, probably thinking that it was poisoned or that something else was amiss. I lit one and handed it to him. Cautiously, he took it from me and began to smoke.

I said "Don't worry" and "OK" repeatedly, as softly and as gently as I could. I don't think he understood any of it, but, after a while, the tone of my voice convinced him that he had nothing to fear.

After finishing his cigarette, he stood up and walked over to the hatch to call down to his wife. She slowly came up and sat down next to him. I offered her a cigarette, but she politely refused.

To a bystander, it would have been a very interesting sight: an American ship captain sitting on an old barge, trying to engage in non-lingual small talk with an old Japanese barge master and his wife; me speaking English, he and his wife using Japanese; neither of us having a spoken word in common, but both of us trying to make the other understand. It doesn't get much stranger than that.

As one would expect, we all began to feel a bit silly and started smiling at each other. After several minutes of intercultural charades, I stood up and started down to the pier, leaving the rest of my Camel cigarettes with my host. He bowed in gratitude for this gift from his guest, who only a few minutes earlier was thought to be an evil conqueror about to kill him.

I had hated the Japanese. I had hated everything about the people who had killed so many of my fellow countrymen in such a terrible war. We were told that the Japanese were evil, sneaky little people who could never be trusted. But it was at that moment, while I was trying to make myself understood to that defenseless old couple, that I realized just how wrong hate is. These two elderly people were as responsible for the war as my own mother was. Were they the enemy? Were they responsible for all the pain and agony that had occurred in the Pacific? No. They were bystanders just like the majority of us. At that moment, the hate I had felt towards the Japanese people (and towards any other people) disappeared.

As I walked down the docks towards my ship, I saw the old man and his wife looking down from the top of their floating home. They waved good-bye to me as though I were an old, dear friend. I returned their wave and headed on my way, never to see them again.

The sun was beginning to set. It was my first sunset in Japan, and the first time since the war had begun that I felt at peace with the world, and with myself.

The Fifth Horseman

IT WAS EARLY EVENING by the time I returned to the 973. My officer of the deck was waiting for me at the bow doors. He told me there was someone who wanted to see me.

An army colonel had stopped by to visit his old command, the 71st Evacuation Unit—the outfit we brought to Yokohama, which we were still in the process of unloading.

The colonel had been transferred to General MacArthur's command at the end of August. His job was to find buildings that the Army could use to treat some of the thousands of wounded Americans still in the Pacific. One of the buildings that the colonel had requisitioned was an elementary school near where we had beached.

In wartime, the relationship between a commander and his men is a close one. I could understand why this fellow felt homesick for his old command.

I invited the colonel to dinner on the ship. One of the advantages of being in the navy instead of the army was that we always had better food. The colonel had been on C and K rations during most of his stay, so I thought he would appreciate a nice, hot meal.

After we sat down for dinner, it didn't take me long to discover that he was a very unhappy man. He seemed tired, like someone who had gotten very little sleep because of some worrying business to which he had to attend.

I asked him why he was so worried, and he looked at me with a rather puzzled expression. "You mean, you haven't heard?"

"Heard what?" I asked.

"Tojo. He shot himself yesterday. And of all the hospitals being set up around here, MacArthur is sending him to *mine*!"

86

He went on to explain that his hospital, a former elementary school, now housed the critically wounded Hideki Tojo. The day before, the former prime minister of Japan had shot himself in the chest at his home in the Setagaya section of Tokyo, just minutes before American military police arrived to take him into custody.

Tojo had attempted to shoot himself in the heart, but the bullet had only grazed one of his lungs. He was rushed to the improvised hospital in Yokohama where, the colonel told me, he was getting the best medical attention the U.S. Army could muster.

The colonel was both haggard and bitter. "I have been getting a nonstop stream of calls and messages from General MacArthur with the same, ominous message: 'THIS MAN MUST NOT DIE!' "

He related some of the details of Tojo's condition and treatment. He also told me that even though he understood the importance of Tojo standing trial for war crimes, he was disconcerted that someone like him should be treated so well.

"I've got GI patients in my hospital. All of them are on regular army cots. This morning, someone brought in a big, old double bed. Guess who it was for? Tojo! An enormous brass studded bed that most of us have dreamed of sleeping in for *years*."

The colonel also told me that General MacArthur had ordered two U.S. Army nurses to be flown in from the Philippines just for Tojo, one for day and one for night. All this extravagance while the rest of the colonel's patients had to survive any way they could. I could understand his frustration and his fear. Douglas MacArthur did not like to be disappointed, especially when it came to a captured foe.

Sometimes in life you are confronted with a strange opportunity and you have to seize it. I had boyhood friends resting on the bottom of the Pacific because of the colonel's patient. What sort of man— what monster—could be responsible for the human misery that had occurred in the Pacific and East Asia? I could not let the opportunity to find out escape me.

I told the colonel that I wanted to see the man responsible for the war that we were both lucky enough to survive. I asked him if I could stop by his hospital and pay a visit to the former prime minister.

He didn't seem surprised by my request, and the hot meal in his stomach had put him in a pretty good mood.

"Sure," he said. "You busy tonight?"

I told him that my OD had things under control and I could leave immediately. After we finished dinner, we hopped into his jeep and headed for the hospital.

It was not difficult to find. What had once been a typical, three-story Japanese middle school, was now a high-security, military prison containing one of the most hated men on Earth. The entire building was lit up like Rockefeller Center at Christmas. Everywhere I looked, guards and military police wore the grim faces of men who would gladly shoot first and ask questions later.

There was much commotion as well—far more noise than would have ever been tolerated at most hospitals. I felt sorry for the American patients who were trying to get some sleep.

The colonel and I drove up to the gate and were automatically allowed to enter. The importance of his patient had made him very well-known to the guards.

We pulled up to the building and walked into the one-time school. The colonel escorted me to the third floor. At the top of the stairs there was a long, darkened hallway, at the end of which were two purposeful-looking soldiers. One stood with a rifle on his shoulder, while the other sat at a desk outside a large double door.

I followed the colonel down the hall. When we reached the orderly's desk, he gestured for me to enter the room. I opened the door and was greeted by one of the two imported nurses. She immediately updated me on the patient's condition in cryptic medical terminology. I quickly told her that I wasn't a doctor, only a visitor. She opened the door wider, beckoned me in, and pointed into the darkness.

There he was. In the far corner of the darkened room, in a big, brass double bed, lay the former wartime prime minister of Japan.

I walked over to the side of the bed, stopping about an arm's reach away. As I approached, a wet, gasping sound broke the silence of the room.

He was a sickly-looking fellow. Occasionally, his eyes would open, roll around in their sockets, then close fitfully, like someone who was having a nightmare.

The moment was hard for me to comprehend. Here, before me, was the man responsible for the deaths of millions and for the pain of millions more in the decades to come. He had once commanded one of the greatest military machines the world had ever seen, and he had used it to decimate entire nations, including his own.

Yet, how insignificant he looked in that bed; how powerless and vulnerable. He looked like just another soldier, from either side of the war, who was near death because of a bullet that had had his name on it.

Tojo's wound was self-inflicted. It was a botched attempt to commit suicide, inflicted minutes before the Americans came to arrest him at his home the previous day. Even though his doctor had marked the spot where the heart is located, the bullet had only grazed the vital organ, seriously damaging a lung—a very painful place to be shot.[5]

It was one of those memorable moments for which we always think we are prepared, but never really are. The nurse, Tojo, and I were surrounded by the silent sound of history that one hears in such circumstances, occasionally interrupted by the distinct, sickening sound of a man who had been shot in the lung. I stood there a few minutes, looking at him and wondering if he was aware of my presence.

My curiosity satisfied, I turned and left. The war was over for him, too.

MacArthur's order would be carried out. Tojo would survive his wound and live to stand trial as a war criminal. Death would come to him, but it would be three years later, on the gallows of Sugamo Prison.

In the hallway, the colonel handed me a sheet of mimeographed paper. "Here. I thought you would like this as a souvenir."

It was the list of all the patients admitted to the hospital within the last twenty-four hours. At the top was the name Tojo, Hideki; occupation: former prime minister of Japan. Better than an autograph, I thought.[6]

The colonel escorted me downstairs and thanked me for dinner. He called for his driver and had me driven back to the ship. We shook hands and he disappeared back into the building, presumably to check on his patient one last time before bed.

As the colonel's jeep drove me back to my ship, I continued the contemplation that had been interrupted by the old man on the barge earlier that day—namely, where my life was going. I realized that I was a fortunate guy who had a lot to be grateful for. Not only had I survived the bloodiest war in history, but within hours of my arrival in the land of my foe, I had met representatives from both the top and the bottom of Japanese society. In a single day I had received an interesting education on the Japanese, or on humanity for that matter. That morning, I had arrived in Japan as a war-hardened and somewhat bitter man. Yet, by the evening, I began to feel at home. Not that Japan was my home, but I felt that the world had come home from a terrible journey that it nearly hadn't survived.

After walking along the shoreline of Yokohama, meeting the old man and his wife, learning that the people of this foreign land were not monsters, and then seeing that the man who had perpetrated the war was mortal as well, I realized that the world's nightmare was really over. A new and better world was going to take its place, and I was going to live to see it happen.

The jeep dropped me off at the bow doors of the 973. I went to the wardroom where I found most of my officers still there. I told them of my meeting with Tojo. None of them believed me until I showed them the colonel's souvenir.

When I got back to my cabin, I fell asleep almost immediately. With the danger of war finally out of my thoughts, I slept better that night than I had in years.

Such was my eventful first day in Japan. At the time, I had no idea that fate was to make it my home, and my life, for the next half-century.

Exit

IT WAS LATE 1945. The war was over and it was time to move on to something else. I was in no hurry to return home to the States. I doubted that I could get my old job at Phelps-Dodge back, and did not like the idea of competing for a job with the millions of other men leaving military service. There were only so many LST captains needed in peacetime.

The peacetime paralysis from which militaries often suffer had already set in. I had been ordered to take up a new command, a floating machine shop in an LST hull called the Romulus. But, by the time I arrived at Pearl Harbor to assume my new post, the ship was back in Yokosuka. I was told that there would be another assignment.

The run-around continued. Suddenly, the Navy had become a large, unwieldy corporation without a mission. It would eventually get reorganized and refocused, but it would take time. While all of this was happening, I had become enamored with Japan. It was an adventure—another adventure—waiting for me. No matter what, I was going to stay.

After making inquiries, I found that there were jobs to be had with MacArthur's occupation government—especially for people with a background in industry. It was my chance. I put in for release from the Navy.

Although the Navy was releasing tens of thousands of men every day, the process was especially complicated for me—almost as complicated as getting in had been. After the usual mountains of paperwork (a miserable job in the days before photocopiers), I was ordered to a hospital ship in Yokosuka to undergo a medical examination.

Ridiculous, I thought. If they found out that I was dying, would they keep me? Still, procedures were procedures and orders were orders.

It was a rather cold and stormy day. Winter would soon be arriving. It wasn't the best time to be aboard a ship, even if it was tied to a pier. Between the sessions of various pokes, prods and the taking of blood, I milled around, chatting with the other patients in a lounge. All of a sudden there was a commotion down the hall. We heard the sound of equipment being overturned, mixed with the sound of shouts and feet in pursuit.

A patient dressed in hospital robes like the rest of us, burst though the door and came tearing into the room. He wore a wild-eyed look, like an animal in terror, sure it was about to die. The man briefly looked around, saw the door that led to the deck, and made for it with several orderlies in hot pursuit. Those of us lounging around, reading magazines, and playing cards dropped everything and followed.

Out on deck it had begun to rain and had gotten very cold. Several of the nurses and orderlies were looking over the side of the ship. The poor fellow had jumped overboard and, it appeared, was trying to drown himself.

Without thinking, I took off my robe and dived into the water. I swam out to the guy and tried to calm him down. He was mad with fright and terror. His head kept dipping below the surface as he tried to push me away and hit me over the head. The water was choppy, the rain was pelting, and this madman was inadvertently trying to drown me. I'd had better days.

Patience does not exist under such circumstances. I belted the fellow across his jaw and he suddenly became very quiet. I grabbed a life preserver that had been tossed from the ship and put him in it. He was quickly hoisted up. Another one was tossed down to me, and I soon followed.

When I made it back on deck I was greeted by several nurses with blankets. Up until that moment, I hadn't felt the cold air or the frigid water. Suddenly I was doubled over. The nurses took me to the showers, tore off my clothes and started to warm me up. Two of the nurses jumped in with me, proceeding to give me the massage of my life, which did a better job of raising my body temperature than hot water ever could.

I stayed on the hospital ship for a few days longer than I had anticipated. The doctors called it observation, but they probably just wanted to see if I had a tendency to act without thinking. For the first time in my life, I was given the title "hero." A few officers stopped by to see me and offer congratulations, telling me I had done a very brave thing. The only problem was that I didn't think before I acted. If I had, I would have never jumped into freezing cold water to save someone. I never did figure out why I did it. I just acted on instinct.

As it turns out, the fellow who almost took his own life had serious mental problems. He was an officer in charge of inventorying equipment and supplies and seeing to their disposal. Yesterday, all the pressure had driven him to the breaking point—a common occurrence after a large scale military exercise like a war. As the old saying goes, it's more dangerous to come down a mountain than to climb one.

While my naval career was winding down, I started spending some of my free time looking up old friends. One of them was my old friend from Annapolis, Willis Manning ("Tommy") Thomas.

I hadn't seen or heard from Tommy since I was running the welding school on Treasure Island. Tommy, who had completed his four years at the Naval Academy, was the captain of a submarine, the U.S.S. Pompano. His boat had arrived in Vallejo for repairs and I drove down to meet him.

We met on the docks next to his sub. We had been young men when we had last set eyes on each other. I had gone on to be a businessman and he had gone to sea. Now, both of us were in a war; he commanded an attack submarine and I trained men to weld.

We spent an entire day together, talking about family, friends, the war, and remembering the past. It was a short period of time, but it will always stand out on my list of good memories.

During lunch, Tommy came up with the idea that I should try to get a transfer to his sub. It was an exciting idea for me. To be together again! To hunt down ships together! He said that he would put in a request for me, and he advised me to formally ask for the transfer. Tommy joked that as he was the one who had introduced me to my wife, Mary, it would give him the chance to make sure that I stayed out of trouble. After all, if anything ever happened to me, Mary would never forgive him.

After a long and exhausting but enjoyable day, I drove Tommy back to the docks. We said good-bye and promised to see each other again soon, hopefully aboard the Pompano. In any event, we would have plenty of stories to tell each other after the war had ended.

My superiors refused my request for a transfer to a sub. Since I had no submarine experience, and men were needed elsewhere, there was no time to send me through school. It was a disappointment I carried with me through the war.

I couldn't wait to see Tommy again. I'm sure that between the two of us we had more sea tales to tell than any other pair in the Navy. Perhaps he had made it to Japan. I always thought the guy could make it to admiral if he was in the Navy long enough. Besides, guys with Tommy's get-up-and-go attitude were bound to do well after the war, regardless of career. I was certain that a great life lay ahead of him.

One day at Yokosuka, I stopped by the part of the base where the submarines berthed. I approached an officer who was just stepping off a boat.

"Excuse me, I'm looking for information on a sub called the Pompano. I'd like to get in touch with her skipper. Do you know someone I could speak to?"

He turned to me in a matter-of-fact manner, as if I were an errand boy taking a message. "The Pompano? Yeah, I know where she is. Her last reported position was off the city of Sendai, not too long before the end of the war. Nobody is really sure, but they think depth charges did her in. Vanished without a trace. All hands presumed dead."

Without another word he walked off towards some nearby buildings. I stood there with the numbness slowly crawling up my spine. The only sound that reached my ears, in one of the world's noisiest naval bases, was that of the waves against the pier on which I was standing.

A quiet moment aboard the
LST-973 while at San Pedro
Bay, Phillippines, 1945.

Navigating aboard GIPSEA, circa 1970.

Playing Santa Claus at St. Luke's hospital in Tokyo, circa 1965.

With President Ronald Reagan.

In the office with Midori.

At my 77th birthday party. From left to right; George Purdy, Mike Mansfield, Admiral Ryohei Oga of the Japanese Maritime Self-Defense Force.

With Ambassador and Mrs. Walter Mondale on the
Fourth of July, 1995.

Receiving the Third Class Order of the Sacred
Treasure from Mayumi Moriyama.

Aboard GIPSEA with Kenichi Horie, one of Japan's most famous adventurers and yachtsmen.

Mother at age 99.

In the office in Tokyo, 1989.

S.C.A.P.

IT WAS A WONDERFUL WAY TO BEGIN the new year. I had my first job outside the military and a title so complicated that few people knew what it meant. There was only one place in Japan that an American with my background could find work: S.C.A.P., short for Supreme Command Allied Pacific.

In 1946, the military-sounding name had very little to do with military matters. Now that the war was over, its job was to rebuild Japan into a new nation that would be peaceful and never again a threat to its neighbors.

My application was accepted faster than I had imagined. Good men with industrial and agricultural backgrounds were needed desperately, especially with the type of experience I had in the metals business. Japan's metal industry had been blown to pieces during the conflict. My job was to get it back on its feet.

My title was Chief of the Metallurgy Branch of the Mining and Geology Division of the Natural Resources Section of S.C.A.P. Basically, my job was to oversee anything that had to do with metals—a broad responsibility given how many different metals are used in industry. Everything from acquisition to inventory came under my jurisdiction. It was a position of much responsibility, and it also put me in direct contact with the captains of what was left of Japanese industry.

I was given a rather sparse office in one of Tokyo's few remaining buildings, close to General MacArthur's headquarters in the Dai-Ichi Insurance Building. I had a staff of one American, a U.S. government expert on mining and metals, and five Japanese, one of whom was a former commander in the Imperial Navy. His name was Hiroyama, a rather unemotional man whose ship sank during the Battle of Okinawa.

At first, there was a level of discomfort in the office. I was part of an occupying force, a conqueror. Such a situation could never be pleasant. But after a few days, everyone began to become accustomed to one another. Yet, from the beginning, I never noticed any animosity on the part of the Japanese. I was their boss and they did what was expected of them.

At that time I didn't speak a word of Japanese, and the staff's level of English was far from fluent. Hiroyama-san was another matter. He was of the old, highly educated class that had brought Japan into the modern world. Although he could not speak a word of English, he was able to read and write the language fluently. During the day, we would sit across from one another in total silence. He would scribble down a message and I would respond by voice, which he had some understanding of, or by note. Such a sight must have looked strange to others, but it worked for us. At least there was a paper trail for everything.

The most fortunate thing about my job was that it required me to travel around Japan inspecting factories and mines. Although I had traveled around the world by ship, I had only seen port cities. It was my first time visiting the interior of another land.

And what a land it was. The first time I saw the Japan Alps, I thought that they were among the most beautiful mountains on earth. The rice fields, remote villages, and temples were, for the most part, untouched by the war. Except for the widespread food shortage, the country seemed fine.

The Japanese were also friendly and kind. They were not the monsters that we had been told about during the war. They were regular people just trying to survive.

On many of my journeys, my companion was a man named Dr. Tokunaga. He worked with Mitsui and Company before the war and was, like me, a specialist in non-ferrous metals. We had a lot to talk about and he was a wonderful tour guide. We would remain good friends for many years.

As one would expect, the U.S. Military controlled everything in Japan, the railroads being no exception. All the trains had special cars reserved for use by the occupation officials. Most of the time they were empty. While on a trip to Kyushu from Osaka, I noticed the car adjacent to ours was packed to the breaking point, mostly with women carrying babies on their backs.

Dr. Tokunaga and I were the only ones in the occupation car. I refused to let those women stand for the next thousand miles. I told Tokunaga that I wanted to invite all the women with children and babies into our car. He understood what I wanted to do, but was apprehensive.

"Purdy-san, you will have to explain everything in great detail. Otherwise, they will not understand. The sign says that the car can only be used for the occupation forces and their staff. They may fear that they will get into trouble."

I reassured my colleague that since we were heading for the end of the line in Kyushu, I wasn't worried about any trouble. Tokunaga went into the next car and took a fair amount of time explaining that it was OK for the mothers with babies and small children to sit down with us. I could see them looking at me from the doorway, as though I was some sort of space creature. After a little coaxing, the majority of the tired women came into our car. They bowed and smiled in our direction, grateful for the rest, as were their children.

Most of the kids who could walk came up to me to check me out. The mothers introduced them by name, and I greeted them by shaking their hands. Soon we were playing games, romping around the car and singing songs. It was on that trip that I learned a couple of Japanese nursery rhymes. The children worked hard to teach me the words, sometimes showing frustration the way an orchestra leader does when a sour note is played. They didn't get angry for long. After all, how often does a young kid have a private train car in which to play.

On that trip I learned the child's game, Scissors, Paper and Stone. It was the first time I had interacted with children since I had left the United States. Most of the mothers smiled the entire time. I suspected that several of them were widows who had not smiled in a long time. They were having as much fun as I was. Dr. Tokunaga, who at first worried that we were breaking some sort of rule, eventually joined in and helped me with my singing. Nobody noticed any railroad personnel looking in through the windows as we snaked our way southward, but I'm sure that the sight of an American official in a railroad car playing with a dozen kids must have set off a few alarms. At the very least, we were the talk of the railroad for the rest of the month.

As we neared Kyushu, the families began to exit the train. Many of the mothers asked for my address in Tokyo. In the weeks to come I would receive letters thanking me for making the trip such a nice one. One of the mothers said that she was very happy that General MacArthur had me as one of his employees.

By the time we arrived in Shimonoseki, all the mothers and kids were gone. As we exited the train and boarded a waiting car that would take us to the factory we were to visit, Dr. Tokunaga gave me a very funny look. He didn't say a word. He just looked at me and then off into the distance, as though he was contemplating something that he wanted to keep to himself. In time, I would learn that the Japanese do not spell out what they are thinking or feeling. What is not said is what matters. For them, the omission carries much relevance. My colleague turned around and gave me a big, broad smile. I guess he had learned something, too.

Grandmother's Attic

ATTICS WERE MADE FOR KIDS. Not just for the ones in between eight and twelve years of age, but for those of all ages. Mysteries are a lot of fun, no matter how old you are.

After dismantling Japan's war machine, one of General MacArthur's first orders of business was to rebuild Japan's economy. That required capital. So, my first job with SCAP was to help figure out how much was left in Japan's till. In addition to having been reduced to a smoldering ruin, the nation was also bankrupt—at least as far as the rest of the world was concerned. The yen was effectively worthless.

Courtesy of the Army Air Corps, Japan's manufacturing base had basically been eliminated. Many of the nation's treasures and cultural assets had been melted down and used to manufacture war material. Countless Japanese artifacts, accumulated over a millennium, had been destroyed in only a few short years.

Japan had also plundered the treasuries of the nations that it had conquered: gold and silver bullion and cultural artifacts from Korea, China, the Philippines and most other Pacific Rim nations under the Greater Eastern Co-Prosperity Sphere.

Much of the treasure has never been accounted for. There are stories of secret places where the Imperial Japanese Army buried tons of gold, silver and other precious metals. One of these tales is of Yamashita's Hoard, supposedly buried in the Philippines. General Yamashita, known as the "Tiger of Burma" in history books, is said to have hidden tons of treasure that was seized from Asian bank vaults during the first years of the war. For fifty years, treasure hunters have been searching in the Philippines and throughout the Far East, looking for Yamashita's Hoard. The buried treasure has remained a mystery comparable to that of Captain Kidd's.

I don't know if any of these stories of Yamashita and his tons of gold, platinum and silver are true, but it gives an idea of the amount of wealth missing by the time the Americans arrived.

My commanding officer ordered me to arrange an inventory of all the precious metals left in Japan. It was to be a complete account of the remaining Japanese spoils of war. It was, for all intents and purposes, a real treasure hunt.

Tokyo's main depository, wherein the Imperial government kept its store of precious metals, was the subterranean vaults of the Bank of Japan. The turn-of-the-century building, located in the Nihonbashi area, was in remarkably good condition, given the amount of devastation that the city had suffered.

It was late morning when I arrived at the bank for the first time. Besides a few guards, there were surprisingly few people. One of the guards greeted me at the curb and escorted me to the office of the colonel in charge of the vaults. Colonel Murry was expecting me and, to my surprise, was quite happy that I had arrived to take charge. "I was told you were coming here," he said in a very relieved tone of voice. "I understand that you are to take inventory, classify, determine the purity of, and the ultimate disposition of, the precious metal items now in our custody."

Although a seemingly competent officer, Colonel Murry's relief stemmed from the fact that he didn't know a lot about precious metals and diamonds. It was three months since the war had ended, and they had only been guarding the place until someone like me arrived. A fortune in gold, silver, jewels, and God knows what else, lay in the middle of a recently hostile city. My guess was that he just wanted to give the burden of keeping track of it to somebody else.

Shortly after we exchanged greetings, the colonel took me down the steps to the basement vault complex. It was a bit dark, since there was little electric power in post-war Tokyo, and very few places were well-lit (power was rationed, much like food). But, it was a neat and clean place. The Japanese had kept the vaults in immaculate condition. The vaults weren't much different than those found in any other part of the world. The only thing out of place was the grim-faced soldiers with carbines, standing around and trying to act nonchalant.

Each vault was assigned a first or second lieutenant, known as a "vault officer." His job was to ensure that nothing left the vault without proper authorization. As I would later find out, it was a more difficult task than most were able to handle.

Several of the vaults contained tons of gold and silver bullion. Much of it still bore the markings of origin: Dutch Indonesia, Hong Kong, Philippines. The Japanese either hadn't bothered to melt it down or they hadn't had the time. Either way, it facilitated the job of returning the stolen property to its rightful owners.

Other vaults contained less obvious treasures that were just as valuable. In one corner, I discovered several wooden barrels. They contained hundreds of slightly shiny pellets about the size of a man's thumb. The colonel didn't know what they were. I could see his surprise when I told him that they were made of pure platinum. Each barrel contained millions of dollars worth of pellets. Anybody could have, and might have, easily walked in and sauntered out with pockets full of platinum.

In other areas I found artifacts that had been taken as spoils of war. At the time I knew little about Asian art, but there were statues that seemed to have come from Korea and China, and vases of pure gold and silver that seemed to have come from Southeast Asia.

There were Japanese treasures as well. I'll never forget the enormous, solid gold sake cup. It was large enough to fit a man, and could have weighed as much as a ton. At the time, it was probably the largest solid gold object in existence. I didn't know what to make of it. However, it turned out to have no historic value. I heard that an association of sake makers had gotten together and constructed it as a promotional gimmick for an international exhibition that was to have been held overseas. Eventually it was returned to the association and, most likely, melted down.

In another corner of the complex were several unmarked, large wooden tea chests. One of the vault officers opened a chest and discovered that it was full of dozens of wax paper rolls, bundled up on both ends. He picked up a roll and began to open it. While doing so, the fragile parcel broke open and what looked like tiny pieces of sugar candy fell out, scattering all over the floor of the vault. Diamonds! Thousands of diamonds! There were enough in one little package to allow a man to live in luxury for his entire life and still have plenty left over for his kids.

Why did the Bank of Japan have so many diamonds? We later learned that during the last few months of the war, the Japanese government had requested that all citizens turn in their jewelry so that the gold and silver could be used in the war effort. Women throughout the country surrendered their wedding and engagement rings, as well as necklaces and brooches. Jewelry studded with diamonds and other precious stones was given to the government to be melted down.

Yet, unless you are fleeing to another country and need to carry a lot of wealth with you, jewels have little value in wartime. The authorities had no use for them, so they separated the diamonds from the precious metal and stored them at the Bank of Japan. It was sad to realize that the hundreds of thousands of engagement rings and other family heirlooms were lost forever. As there was no hope of returning them to their rightful owners, they were later sold to department stores and jewelry merchants for resale. Today, some of the rings in a the fashionable shops on the Ginza in Tokyo probably contain some of these wartime diamonds.

It was a real treasure house; something straight out of Hollywood. Over the nest several months I spent many hours at the vaults, counting billions of dollars worth of booty.

One of the lessons that I had learned early in life, and one that I applied during my inventory duties at the Bank of Japan, was that one should always have an alibi. If one ever finds himself in a situation in which he has access to enormous riches, he should never allow himself to be left alone with it. It's not to keep himself honest, but to ensure that he will not be suspected of thievery if someone else isn't honest. No matter what the governments says about "innocent until proven guilty," when it comes to gold bullion, the mere suspicion of theft is enough to ruin your career, or even your entire life. Each visit to the Bank of Japan vaults, I made sure that someone was with me at all times. I always had a witness to vouch for what I did and didn't touch. Future events would prove it to be a wise precaution.

No security system is completely secure. Even though SCAP took every reasonable precaution to ensure that no precious metals were stolen by American soldiers, some valuables did end up missing. One of my duties was to work with the military police, tracking down people who had put their hands into Japan's national cookie jar.

One case involved finding the origin of some silver rings that had suddenly appeared on the fingers of U.S. Army personnel based at Camp Drake, just outside of Tokyo. A cavalry regiment was based there.

After surviving the war, everyone felt a strong bond with the unit in which they had served. Items bearing the unit insignia were always sought after by members. Usually, they had the insignia engraved on a Zippo lighter or tattooed on a forearm. Yet, for some reason, beautifully engraved, solid silver rings started showing up at Camp Drake. Silver was not readily available to the general public, so suspicion was raised.

The rings appeared to have been made out of rolled sheet silver, a substance that, under the laws of occupation, individuals were not permitted to own. The Military Police called me in to help figure out from where it came, and, if a hoard of silver was discovered, to identify its origin.

After questioning soldiers who were found to be in possession of the rings, the police learned of a house near Camp Drake that seemed to be the source of the illicit rings.

Early one morning, I went with the U.S. Military and Japanese police to pay a visit to the house. It was, for want of a better word, a raid. The man who greeted us at the door was notably nervous, especially when one of the Japanese cops showed a ring, but he continued to deny any knowledge of them.

We sat down and had a polite conversation with the fellow, until it became obvious he was hiding something. The police searched the place for a couple of hours, but found nothing until they discovered a trap door in the kitchen. Underneath, there was a well-provisioned ring factory, along with two tons of sheet silver. We discovered another sizable hoard buried in the back yard. I compared it to the rings and, sure enough, we had our man. We sent the fellow to the clink and the metal was confiscated.

There were other incidents and raids, but the one that was the most sensational, and the most unfortunate, was the one that involved the man in charge of security at the Bank of Japan vaults: Colonel Murry. S.C.A.P. had selected Colonel Murry to be the custodian of all the wealth contained in the Bank of Japan's vaults. A member of the prestigious Army Corps of Engineers, Murry had served with distinction during the war. He was a very personable and likable fellow. He had survived the conflict and had a terrific future ahead of him.

The Occupation Government had spent a fair amount of time looking for the right guy to guard the piggy-bank. They were extremely selective. The job required someone with an impeccable record, because of the opportunity to mishandle things. From a long list of candidates, they picked him for the job. There's an old saying that diamonds are a girl's best friend, but to a thief they can be his worst enemy. To the people in the business, diamonds are as individual as works of art are to a gallery. Just like paintings, there are well-known diamond masterpieces whose identifying marks are kept on file at most of the world's major jewelry stores. These files are used when stones are known to be stolen or missing.

Not too long after the end of the war, some very peculiar diamonds appeared at jewelry stores in the San Francisco Bay Area. Many of the stones were quite large and, during the war, had been recorded as missing. One stone in particular, and the one that would later prove to be the thief's undoing, was a stone with historical significance.[7] The FBI was immediately called in to investigate, probably because Nazi war criminals who had fled Europe were known to have been using diamonds to finance their escapes.

An investigation into the source of the diamonds pointed to Colonel Murry's wife, who lived near San Francisco. Evidently, she had been selling diamonds, in quantity, to jewelry outlets in the area. The Feds quickly discovered the identity of Mrs. Murry's husband and what he did for a living. But, since selling diamonds was not a crime, the authorities needed proof that he was stealing them from Japan and shipping them back home. Californian diamond merchants were given a description of Mrs. Murry and told to buy any diamond she offered. The government would compensate the expenses. The investigation, and diamond sales, lasted for about six months.

While the FBI secretly investigated Murry and his wife, Murry got his orders to return home. After transferring his command, he packed his belongs and boarded a ship in Yokohama. When he stepped off the ship in San Francisco, he was greeted at the bottom of the gangplank by two men in suits.

"Excuse me, sir, are you Colonel Murry?"

He was in civilian clothes instead of his uniform. He answered in the affirmative. They identified themselves as Federal Agents and escorted him to a nearby office. Inside, he saw all of his luggage. Murry was asked if the luggage belonged to him and if he had anything else to declare to U.S. Customs. He told the men that he had declared everything and he didn't object when they asked to open his bags and search his pockets.

Murry's possessions were thoroughly searched, but no diamonds were discovered. The colonel was even subjected to a body search, but nothing out of the ordinary was discovered. They were about to give up and release him, when one of the customs agents discovered that Murry's watch had stopped. A rather large pocket watch was dangling on the chair on which Murry had placed his clothes,. "Well, Colonel, here's one thing you forgot," one of the agents said, as he held it for all to see.

"That's a keepsake, an heirloom from my grandfather," Murry replied. The agent asked Murry if it ran, and was told it hadn't for a long time. "Maybe some day I'll see if I can get it fixed," he said.

One of the customs agents opened the back of the watch, and the jig was up. Inside, there were several choice diamonds. He was arrested, held for a time, and then sent back to Japan to stand trial.

The military police interrogated everyone who had had anything to do with Murry, and I was no exception. I had spent a fair amount of time with the man and had worked closely with him, but I never had any idea he was stealing diamonds. Fortunately, I was never in the vaults without an escort, so I was quickly cleared of any suspicion.

Murry was court-martialed, convicted, and sent to San Quentin prison in California. He served about five years in prison before being paroled. I learned later that he got a job as an engineer in a small California town.

In the late-1950s, I was in California on business and decided to look up my one-time associate. I drove to the small town in which he had settled and found his house. It was a typical bungalow with a little porch three or four steps up from the sidewalk. I got to the front door and rang the bell. An elderly lady answered, who turned out to be Mrs. Murry. I'd never seen her before, and she'd never seen me. She opened the door, but kept the screen door latched.

"Good afternoon. Are you Mrs. Murry?

She said, "Yes."

I said, "Well, my name is George Purdy. I'm an old friend of Colonel Murry's." As soon as I said "Colonel Murry," she backed off a little bit and, notably shaken, said "Where did you know my husband?"

I told her that I had known him in Japan. I could feel the tension and see her tremble.

"Just a moment."

She went back inside and, a few minutes later, the colonel came to the door. I've never seen such a big change in a man. He didn't look, he didn't act, and he didn't seem anything like the man who had been a bird colonel in the army. The moment he saw me, he started to cry.

He opened the screen door and invited me in. I was at a loss for words. I had come all that way, and I couldn't think of a thing to say.

I blurted out, "Colonel, how are you feeling these days?"

He replied, "Well, I'm not too good. You can see I've lost a lot of weight and this experience has made a different man of me. I can say that to you because you know what it was."

I said, "Yes, but I didn't come here to talk about that, Colonel. I just came over to say hello and to tell you again how much I enjoyed and appreciated knowing you.

He started to cry again. His wife got up and left the room. After about five minutes, I thought that I should leave. I was digging up something that they were trying to bury.

We talked for ten or fifteen minutes more, mostly about his job as an engineer with the city, and then I said, "Well, I have to go. I'm driving back to San Francisco. Colonel, I just wanted to say hello and give you my best wishes."

He escorted me to the door, and we said good-bye. He and Mrs. Murry thanked me for coming to see them.

About three months after my visit to his home, Colonel Murry died. Although what he did was wrong, I don't think of the man as a real criminal. He was just a man, a good man, who gave in to temptation and paid the price for the rest of his life. If anything, Colonel Murry was just another tragic casualty of World War II.

The age-old rule for children also applies to adults: you can play around in Grandmother's attic, just don't take any of Grandmother's things.

Hanging the Shingle

BEING A GOVERNMENT EMPLOYEE has its advantages, but only if the government is going to be around for a while. The United States would not occupy Japan forever. If I was going to stay, I had to strike out on my own.

While in S.C.A.P., I had made a significant number of contacts in Japanese industry. I knew the heads of the bigger companies and had worked with them to rebuild the country. While I was with the occupation government, I didn't tell anyone that I planned to start my own company after I left, but they all knew I planned to stay in Japan. Many told me that they looked forward to further contact with me "later on."

On January 1, 1949, the day after I left S.C.A.P., I hung out my shingle. Soon after, George I. Purdy & Company was formally incorporated. My career in the business world had begun.

During the occupation, trade was the only business that a foreign resident of Japan could get into. Everything was needed: food, clothing, supplies of all sorts and, especially, money. The Japanese were desperate to earn currency in order to rebuild their economy. Thus, many import/export companies came into being. A great many of these firms were run by foreigners like myself—men who wanted to grow rich with the country.

Running a business is not very different from running a ship. Unlike the Navy, where I was trained to know everything about every job that I was assigned, I was hopelessly unprepared for what awaited me in the world of commerce. I had to learn many new skills without help. Letters of credit, foreign exchange and control, and all the ins and outs of commodity trade were new to me. It was

116

a long uphill battle, but I didn't have a choice. If I were to stay in Japan, it was all I could do for a living.

In the beginning, I made enough to survive, scraping by from month to month. After I left S.C.A.P., I had to move out of my plush quarters at the Dai-Ichi Hotel and into a fairly small apartment. I then moved into a partial occupancy house in the Ichigaya section of the city. It was a nice place that had survived the war. A Japanese family lived in the Japanese part of the house, while I lived in the Western section. They were nice to me and often invited me to dinner. It was a good way to learn the language, as well as the lifestyle, of the people who were my customers.

That first year was difficult, but as 1950 began, things were looking up. I was learning the virtues needed to succeed in Japan, patience being at the top of the list. I was also earning a reputation for honesty and reliability—something that would save me many times.

It was easy for me to interact with people in both a business and a social setting. From the time I was very young, my parents instilled in me the importance of living honestly and working hard. However, many others did not abide by the code.

I made a contract with an iron ore producer in Southern California, which gave me the distribution rights for their product in Japan, provided that I invested in the company. On paper it was a sweet deal. Business had been going well, and I had accumulated some money over the past year. I made the investment and was part owner of an iron ore operation.

I turned to a Japanese trading company with which I had done some business, asking them help me distribute the ore. The president of A. Takahashi & Company had become a good friend and worked with me on the project. Using his connections with the Japan Steel Producers Association, he sold some ten thousand tons of iron ore. We signed the contracts and waited for the ships to arrive.

We only saw two thousand tons. The U.S. company had gone

bankrupt. The money I had invested was gone. Suddenly, I found myself with a debt of one million yen—a significant amount of money in 1950.[8]

It was a very embarrassing and trying experience. Mr. Takahashi also lost money in the deal, not to mention his credibility. He had had strong links to the steel people, who also had problems because their production, and subsequent delivery, was also thrown off. He suffered because of a deal that I had brought to him. The fault was sitting squarely on my shoulders.

It was the biggest catastrophe of my life. My whole future was hanging in the balance. I needed one million yen. I had no collateral and, given what had just happened, no credit. Desperation is a horrible thing, especially if one is alone.

The only people to whom I could turn were my friends at NSK, a ball and roller bearing manufacturer that I had dealt with during my S.C.A.P. days. The general manager of the company was Horimoto-san, a man with whom I had kept in contact after starting my own business. I gave him a call, went over to meet them, and explained the situation. I then asked for a loan.

By its nature, lending money is a dangerous thing—borrowing it is as well. The folks at NSK sat down with me and politely, but seriously, asked me questions about my business. They explained to me that they were not a bank and that capital was almost as precious a commodity as rice. I told them that I understood but that there was nowhere else I could go. They told me that they would consider the matter and get back to me in a couple of days.

At such times, a death wish creeps into a man's head. The inability to control one's life, one's fate, is a hell like none other. I had worked hard to get to this point. I had sacrificed a great deal as well. If they did not approve the loan, I would have no choice but to file for bankruptcy and return to the United States, where an uncertain future awaited me, as a failure.

I lived next to my office telephone for the next seventy-two hours. Many times I picked up the receiver from the cradle, wanting to call, but knowing that it would not work. The people at NSK would not want to see desperation.

Finally, the phone rang. It was Horimoto-san. He asked me to come to the office right away. Apprehensive, I ran across town to their office, dodging, and nearly hitting, many lunchtime pedestrians along the way.

In the office of the general manager, a stack of money was sitting on a meeting table: one million yen. Next to the money, there was a letter written in English on NSK stationary. It was a receipt for the money, explaining that I agreed to repay the entire amount at my earliest convenience. There was no mention of interest.

I signed the receipt and put the money into my briefcase. I thanked everyone in the room for their generosity and kindness. It was the first time since I had arrived in Japan that I bowed to someone and really meant it. A few years earlier, these people had been a hated enemy. Now, they were subjects of a foreign power. They had seen me make a stupid business mistake. Yet, they were helping me.

I went back to my office, closed the door, and sobbed.

Saved by the Cannon

1950 WOULD REMAIN A YEAR of problems. It took me three months—three backbreaking months of round-the-clock, seven-day-a-week trading—to repay NSK. The family with whom I was living never saw me and probably thought that I had moved out.

By the end of the year, I had my life in order. I needed a change, and one was made for me. North Korea, backed by the Soviet Union, had invaded South Korea, backed by the United States. The first shooting match of the Cold War had begun.

At such times of crisis, companies often want someone in or near the country to keep an eye on their interests. One such firm was Philadelphia-based Woodward & Dickerson, dealers in chemical fertilizers. They had heard of me through the grapevine and asked my company to continue servicing their customers in Korea during the conflict. It was much needed, steady, dependable business. We took the contract, excluding almost all other business.

In spite of the blood being spilt on the peninsula, I never saw nor ever came close to a battle. Amazing as it may seem, farmers never stopped buying fertilizer. Even with the threat of millions of Chinese taking over, they kept growing food.

During the war, I made many trips to Korea. Sometimes, I went three or four times a week. At that time, one of the more popular intra-Asian airlines was Civil Air Transport of the Republic of China (Taiwan). I almost always used them. They gave me a special deal because I was such a regular passenger—probably the first in their history. I flew so many miles with them that, during one of their anniversary parties held in Tokyo near the end of the war, they gave me a silver letter opener. I was their most traveled customer during the Korean War.

Although I never witnessed any fighting, it was after the war that business became dangerous.

My time in Korea had made me known to the U.S. Government employees who were helping the native population clean up the mess caused by the three years of war. The Office of Procurement for the Republic of Korea, better known as OPROK, was set up with U.S. assistance and money so that the massive quantities of raw materials needed to rebuild a nation would be more easily managed and controlled.

Wars and occupations always result in bitterness, which can appear to be petty and ridiculous, but is often understandable. In 1954, the Koreans were angry at many people: not just their fellow countrymen with whom they had fought a civil war, but with the Japanese who had occupied them, often brutally, since 1910.

Syngman Rhee was the first post-Korean-War/Japanese occupation president of the Republic of Korea. There was no man who hated the Japanese more than he did. He wanted no contact with the former colonial power that ruled over his country for thirty-five years. It was illegal to speak the Japanese language in the ROK, even in an airplane flying over the country. Few Japanese were permitted into the country. Neither Japan nor Korea recognized each other. Diplomacy between the two countries was nonexistent.

The attitude towards the Japanese extended to all aspects of trade. Nothing that originated in Japan was allowed into the country. There were few exceptions, one of which was chemical fertilizer provided by the Far East agent of Woodward & Dickerson.

Although the U.S. Government was sympathetic to Rhee and to the Koreans' hatred of their former rulers, hatred didn't accomplish much. Korea needed many resources and semi-manufactured goods to rebuild its economy. Japan was its next door neighbor. To not trade with the country was foolish, not to mention expensive. It was also dangerous. In the months following the cease-fire with the North, the Eisenhower government was anxious to calm North Asia. Having Japan and Korea openly hostile to each other while the Soviet Union and Communist China were on the move was giving the people in Washington nightmares.

One day, while in Seoul, I met retired Colonel Andrew Divine. The colonel told me that he had a business proposition that he hoped I would find attractive. He said that the U.S. Government wanted someone to break the boycott of Japanese goods in the Korean market. Since I was already selling in Korea, and selling to OPROK, they wanted to help me win a contract to supply Japanese-made cement and steel reinforcing rods.

Others had tried and failed, but this time was different. The Koreans were purchasing these materials from France and elsewhere at substantially higher costs than they could get them for on their side of the Sea of Japan. The U.S. taxpayer was subsidizing this hatred, and the people in Washington wanted it to end. Yet, the Americans couldn't publicly force the Koreans to change their practices. They needed someone else to do their work for them.

I agreed to get a Japanese company to provide me with an offer. I would be the middleman in the deal. I was in for the ride of my life.

Without my knowledge, I had been chosen to be the instrument of U.S. foreign policy. Washington had directed the colonel to approach me and use me to try to break the Korean boycott. Geopolitics were at play and I was in the middle of them.

Such a plan, and a contract, required the support of the entire Japanese industry. I returned to Tokyo and met with the senior members of the Cement and Steel Manufacturers Associations. At first, they didn't believe me. There had been previous attempts, but all had failed. I was a well-known businessman in Tokyo. When the going got tough, I stayed in place and fixed what was broken. If I had not gone through such an experience, they probably wouldn't have given me the hearing.

Japan's steel and cement producers wanted nothing more than

to sell to Korea, yet the edict of President Rhee was standing in their way. Few in the business believed that things could change anytime soon.

I proposed a deal that would give my company exclusive rights to the sale of all Japanese cement and steel if, and only if, I was the first to win an OPROK contract. That was the deal.

The members of the associations were surprised at my request, but quickly decided that they had nothing to lose. After all, nobody else had told them that it was possible to break the boycott. A verbal agreement, sufficient in the Japan of the time, was made.

The OPROK Invitation to Bid number was 49. It was for ten thousand tons of cement and four thousand tons of steel reinforcing rods. We assembled the necessary documentation. It had to be airtight, without errors or omissions, or a reason to disqualify it might arise. We submitted the bid and began to wait. It didn't take long before things got hot.

As I look back now, I would have loved to have been a fly on the wall of the office that first looked at our bid and saw that the supplier was in Japan. It must have caused a commotion, because the authorities had a sudden interest in me. I had heard horror stories of police coming into the offices of companies that had tried to do the same thing, often tearing apart the facilities for the seeming joy of it. I requested, and was provided with, protection by the U.S. authorities. Twenty-four hours a day, an Army jeep and two MPs were at my beck and call. I was told not to leave my hotel unless I had an escort. I had upset the Korean apple cart.

First, I received a visit from Korean Immigration officials. They said that they wanted to look at my passport. I pulled it out and showed it to them from a distance, not letting their fingers anywhere near it. They bullied and threatened me, but I just stood there, trying to look like stone. After about an hour of being unpleasant, they left. I got on the phone to Colonel Divine and asked for the MPs. Every day, we would have lunch at his hotel. He would then give Washington an update on my progress.

Next came the tax authorities. They showed up without warning, proceeding to examine every scrap of paper in the place. They said that they had received information that something was being hidden in the office. After a few visits, they tired of the game and passed to the next team.

One morning, a frantic phone call from our Korean fertilizer distributor made it clear what we were up against. He told me that police had torn their office apart. Nobody wanted to see a Japanese company win this contract.

The terror lasted fifteen days. Finally, one of the top people at OPROK with whom I had dealt with on other contracts paid me a visit at my besieged office. At first, he was very straightforward and demanding, then he changed to a conciliatory tone.

"Mr. Purdy, please, *please* withdraw your bid."

I replied that I couldn't do that. It was a viable business deal and I saw no problems with it. I sat there and let the words sink in.

The next day, after much drama and commotion, OSROK (Office of Supply)—not OPROK—accepted the bid. The organization had changed its name from the time I submitted my bid until the time it was awarded. At first, it appeared to be a sticking point, but in the end it was ignored.

I couldn't believe my luck. After the tender was accepted, Colonel Divine invited me over to his local hotel for a drink. He congratulated me and then pulled a telegram out of his pocket and handed it to me. "I didn't want to tell you about this until *after* the contract was awarded," he said with a wink.

The cable was from the State Department of Commerce in Washington. It said that if my bid was reasonable and competitive *and* wasn't awarded, the ROK government would be told that all aid, excluding military aid, would immediately be stopped.

I was shocked; the colonel smiled. As it would turn out, the deal would pave the way for a flood of commercial activity between the two nations and, eventually, the restoration of diplomatic ties.

The deal was also a turning point in my life. I was to be the sole source of Japanese steel and cement to Korea. The Cement and Steel Associations kept their word, without any paper to remind them of the fact.

I had made it into the big leagues. There was no doubt in my mind as to where I would live for the rest of my life.

Pinnacle

OVER THE COMING YEARS, my life would get better and better. I would have my ups and my downs, but it was a good ride.

Mary and I were divorced early on during the first years in Japan. She didn't enjoy the Asian lifestyle as much as I did. Mary was far more comfortable with life in the United States and wanted to make El Paso her home. We had spent many years apart and, in the interim, had grown in different directions. So, sadly, we parted ways.

The day she left our home in Tokyo, the entire neighborhood lined the streets to say farewell to her and to my young son, William, as they headed back to the United States. It was one of the darkest days of my life.

In the ensuing years, she and I would remain in contact as friends. We had been through a lot together, and our experiences had made us better people.

Yet, every ending leads to a beginning. Midori, a woman who is one of the best friends I have ever had, became my wife in 1963. Since then, we have lived a wonderful life together. We enjoy life to its fullest and not a day goes by that we aren't grateful for having found each other among all the other people in the world.

Boating is a passion that Midori and I share. We were the proud owners of two custom-built cabin cruisers named GIPSEA.[9] Over the years, we have had the honor of having many notable people aboard as our guests: politicians, ambassadors, business executives, and friends in the Japanese Maritime Defense Force and the United States Navy. Maintaining a boat was a lot of work, but it made the time away from business much more enjoyable.

126

Being successful in business can be a joy, but there are other places to focus one's efforts. I always found the time to work with various charities and nonprofit organizations in Japan. Among them were the Boy Scouts, an organization I helped re-establish in Japan after World War II. Since I became involved in 1952, I have been awarded the honors of the Silver Beaver and the Silver Antelope. There are few things I value as highly.

I have dedicated a great deal of time to Japan's Navy League, an organization that has improved relations between the various U.S. and Japanese military branches operating in the country. One of the most productive organizations with which I have been affiliated is the American Chamber of Commerce in Japan, which elected me as its president in 1972. Over the years, I would be involved in many activities aiming to foster the links between the U.S. and Japanese economies.

My business grew and expanded until I sold it to Dresser Industries in 1965. I remained as head of the Japan operations until mandatory retirement at age sixty-five, more than a quarter of a century ago. Yet, I did not retire from business, and I have no plans to do so.

I have continued as a member of the board of directors of Dresser Japan. Midori and I still control several different business enterprises and we plan to have even more. I still visit the office a couple of days a week, and keep up to date on the business in Tokyo and in the rest of the world. I have learned that keeping the mind and body active and alert does more for one's life span than any other tonic or elixir.

Although it has been a busy life, and business has occupied so many years of it, I still take the time for a regular walk on the marina that Midori and I call home. I listen to the waves beat against the shore and the dikes. Sometimes, as the sun slowly sets on the ocean, bathing the surrounding houses in an orange-gold, I reflect on my life. Everything that I set out to do has been reasonably accomplished. In these quiet moments of contemplation,

127

I think of dreams that never faded and never left me disappointed or wanting more.

It all began for me on a remote island in a remote place in the past, and it never ended. I have always lived on the same pond; I just built my home on a different shore.

All Ashore

WHEN THEY MADE A MOVIE about the place, they called it "Sands of Iwo Jima." I had a problem with that title. The place has no sand, only gritty, volcanic dirt. To me, sand was always something pleasant; a substance that made my feet feel good while walking on it, especially if it was wet. The tiny little dot in the Pacific, whose name means "Island of Sulfur" in Japanese, wasn't pleasant. The blackness took in the heat from the sun, making for an environment similar to that inside a pressure cooker. It was not a nice place to visit and certainly not a nice place to live.

Nor was it enjoyable half a century earlier to the soldiers of two armies. Their murderous fistfight has gone down in history as one of the bloodiest ever. Now, the young men are all old. The survivors of both sides were invited to the remote island where they had almost been killed. Many came with their children. Some came in wheelchairs. Others came alone. Many were happy, many were sad. Some were still angry.

Although I had nothing to do with the history of the island, I was invited to the ceremonies marking the fiftieth anniversary of the Battle of Iwo Jima, and asked to be part of the Japanese delegation. As an American veteran who had fought on the other side, it was an honor like few others I have ever received.

It was a long, one-day event, requiring all the Japanese participants to rise early in the morning. Most of the flights to Iwo left before dawn, requiring people to stay in hotels near the American and Japanese military bases whence the aircraft would originate.

The Americans had a longer way to go. They made their way to

129

the U.S. Territory of Guam, where they boarded chartered flights to the island.

Unlike when it had been a battlefield, the island was covered with lush vegetation. Many areas were covered with the eerie green associated with the tropics. In the ensuing years, Iwo Jima had been taken over by the Japanese military and was regularly used by the U.S. Navy to practice carrier landings. The veterans arriving as guests probably found it unnerving that American marines and Japanese naval personnel were working together to coordinate the events. Their day to remember a horrible battle was being managed by the grandchildren of both sides.

Like the other VIPs, I was shepherded around throughout the day. I was escorted around the party to meet with various people, American and Japanese. We were taken on a tour of the island and shown the places where men had fought and died over something to which the historians have yet to give a logical reason. Perhaps someday they will, but I doubt it.

The big event was a memorial service held at a spot overlooking the invasion beaches. A memorial, inscribed in English and Japanese, would be dedicated. The U.S. Ambassador to Japan, Walter Mondale, a former vice president, gave the most moving speech. He told the crowd and assembled press corps that what had once been a sea of death had been transformed into something peaceful. Where ships of war once plied the waters, those of commerce now move freely between nations. Peace should be appreciated and guarded, and the way it came about remembered.

Joining him at the podium after his address was the widow of the Japanese garrison commander of the island, who had died during the battle. She was bent and slow-moving from her years, but had made the long trip to sit out in the broiling sun with the rest of us. Mondale put his arm around her, as tears welled up in his eyes. It was a gesture that was appropriate to the intimacy of the moment. Pain and loss are universal concepts that transcend nations and boundaries. Peace and prosperity are as well.

130

As the former enemies began to shake hands and talk about the hell they had once shared, and as long-lost comrades were reunited for the first time since their youth, I noticed something offshore.

Several large whales were at play, "breaching," as it is called. Those enormous and graceful creatures would leap into the air and then crash back into the water. It was a beautiful sight, one of nature at its best.

I remembered the whales that had frolicked in the waves offshore of another island many years ago. In my mind, I returned to that place—that summer—that would change my life and serve as a reference point for all that came after. Since then the world had changed greatly, yet the sea had remained the same. It sounded and smelled the same, still holding the level of mystery, danger and adventure that had attracted me, as it will attract the many others who will follow.

The whales seemed to be enjoying themselves. I wished that I could have joined them.

You're only as old and miserable as you want to be. It's as true for nations as it is for individuals.

Epilogue

I THINK MOST PEOPLE who spend their lives as expatriates never planned to do so. Living the majority of your years away from the land of your birth is a lot like falling in love, it sort of happens when you aren't looking for it or expecting it. You have to let it come in its own time and accept all that happens.

I have been very fortunate. I've sailed the world, served in a war, and lived to tell the tale. I've been blessed with a loving, supportive wife and many good friends who have helped me without question when I needed it. These are the two most wondrous treasures that one can ever possess.

One of the nice things I've discovered about writing a biography is that you can leave your thoughts and ideas behind for posterity to ponder. I've always made it a point to speak my mind at the appropriate time, so here it goes:

Although there are many doomsayers who believe that the best days of Japan are behind her, I think that my adoptive nation has many great years ahead. I saw an entirely defeated nation rise like a phoenix from the ashes of World War II, and survive to become one of the most prosperous nations in the history of the world. I saw a people accept total defeat and subjugation and bear it with dignity. The people I once considered my enemy became some of the best friends of my life. A country that can overcome so much and come so far after getting knocked down so badly can accomplish anything it sets its mind to.

For those of you who have your own business, or just want to succeed in whatever you do, remember to always keep your nose clean. Emphasize honesty and integrity in everything you do. Live by this rule, and you will never have to apologize for words or actions.

Now, for those who say that honesty is a naive, simplistic or out-dated value, I'd argue that it makes good business sense. You'd be surprised how that little rule can add to your productivity as well as add years to your life. For decades, doctors have been saying that stress will kill you. Yet, few doctors point out that the worst kind of stress is incurred by doing something wrong and then trying to live with the guilt. Peace of mind is priceless.

Honesty may be difficult at times, given the kind of people we have to deal with on a day-to-day basis. Everyone has something he or she is ashamed of but if you keep your life, both business and professional, honest and clean, you will never have to look over your shoulder to see who's there, or jump with surprise if someone taps you on the shoulder. I've heard of businessmen who made heaps of money from dishonest work, only to die prematurely due to the stress of possibly being found out. If you work at it, there are plenty of honest ways to make money. Business is more fun if you can get a good night's sleep.

You should also emphasize sincerity and reliability in your work. Never pretend to have knowledge of something with which you are unfamiliar. I've seen so many people, so many times, try to "bull" their way through a situation. The minute they get found out, they're finished. Exaggeration is a dangerous and unprofitable exercise.

I've often been asked the secret of successfully managing people. The "secret" is not much of a secret. My only edge is that I became a manager at a relatively early age, and during a time when machines in the office were not the biggest asset—people were.

Never forget that people are your single most important asset *and* responsibility. Encourage and answer questions. The people who work for you are human beings and much of their happiness and fulfillment in life depends on you. Show an interest in their welfare. Let them know that they are more than cogs in a machine.

Don't be too restrictive to your young employees. Breathing down someone's neck doesn't create a good worker. Instead of restricting your employees, work with them. Teach them and encourage them. Don't order them around like servants. It's your job to get them to

133

think for themselves. Be as free with your compliments as you are with your admonitions. It's human nature to be critical, but it's something that can be overcome. Too many of us criticize more than we compliment. Overcome the instinct.

In addition to treating your employees well, always remember that there are two things that can make or break a businessperson: not saying "no" often enough and not constantly asking "why?" of your subordinates.

There are endless business opportunities that will come your way. If you grab at all of them, you won't catch any of them. No matter how great the temptation, you have to let most opportunities pass. I've seen many people lose everything because they never mastered the use of the word "no." Learn how to pronounce it, spell it and say it. If necessary, practice it in front of a mirror. It will be the secret of your success.

The reason for asking "why?" is simple. Everything has an answer, so only a fool isn't constantly asking the question. By asking why something is or isn't working, is or isn't making money, or is or isn't operating properly, you will not only have the people in your organization on their toes (and at their best), but you'll also learn a hell of a lot. After all, the human race invented formalized education to answer the timeless question of "why?", so use this process to make your company run better.

The rules for being an employee are simple: work like hell and don't take advantage of those who are nice to you. Misinterpreting good treatment as a sign of weakness is a stupid thing to do. An employer who treats his employees well is doing a good job. If his company was made up of weaklings, it wouldn't last for long. Don't ever take advantage of someone who is nice to you; they may stop.

Although work or business is a necessity of life, we can't separate ourselves from the world around us and spend our days just making money. Everyone must take an active role in what happens to our little blue planet. This role should include participating in public affairs. Over the last couple of decades, many younger people, in Japan and in the United States, have taken a less active role in the political process. This development is rather dangerous and must be reversed.

To borrow from Ronald Reagan, communism may be on the ash heap of history, but we still live in a very dangerous world. My generation learned the hard way that dictators and tyrants cannot be appeased. Wish as we might, they don't listen to reason. They never have and they never will. Just like weeds, they'll continue to pop up everywhere.

Paying money to potential enemies, usually in the form of foreign aid or "loans," doesn't work either. If you walk up to someone on the street and say "Hi! I'd like to be your friend. Here's one hundred dollars," you won't get a friend. What you will get is someone who will soon be trying to get one thousand dollars out of you. Most of us know that money doesn't buy happiness; it doesn't buy friendship either.

Many of the mistakes that the United States made earlier in this century are being repeated. Although the Soviet Union is gone, we no longer have the ability to project our power and come to the aid of our allies in a time of crisis. The sad state of the U.S. merchant fleet is the best example of this neglect. Getting rid of the Merchant Marine was one of the worst errors the United States ever made. We have lost our ability as a nation to manufacture ships on a large scale and, given the fact that we are surrounded by the world's two largest oceans, we will someday pay the price for this oversight. If there is a major global conflict during the coming decades, loading up the aircraft that we have at our disposal, along with men and materials, may not be enough to stop another tyrant. As Desert Storm showed us, ships are still an important part of any effective armed forces.

During World War II, we were able to call on a large reserve of civilian merchant vessels to use in the war effort. At the beginning of the war, our substantial merchant marine also gave us the ability to induct men into the Navy who were already trained seamen—saving us valuable months and the lives of countless people living in the path of the Axis powers.

Like it or not, our planet is mostly covered with water and, for the foreseeable future, that fact doesn't seem to be changing. The oceans are still the highways by which most of the world's commerce travels. Many of the products that we no longer manufacture come to us by sea. Only a madman would live on an island and not keep his shipbuilding skills up to date.

Although the U.S. is under a crushing burden of debt, we must remember that accountants do not win wars. During World War II we did not worry about cost. If we had preoccupied ourselves with budgets, Berlin would have become the capital of Europe, and the people of Japan probably never would have had the opportunity to learn about freedom and democracy. When engaged in a fight for survival, one worries about the economic concerns later. It's possible to get out of debt through hard work; getting out of a grave is another matter.

In our endeavor to save money in the short term, we have set out on a path that will cost future generations more money if they need to replace the power we used to have. We cannot plan our defenses by only looking to the needs of the next couple of years. It must be a long-term strategy that will keep our true friends and us safe. It will also keep our books balanced.

Without strong armed forces, our form of democracy could prove to be responsible for its own undoing. History repeats itself, and it frightens me that, only a few years after the end of the Cold War, the United States' moves towards drastically reducing our military are weakening us to the role of a second-rate power. We did the same thing in the 1930s and our weakness largely contributed to the tragedy of World War II.

Every young man and woman should be exposed to military discipline for one or two years. This exposure is especially necessary for a democracy that believes in individual rights. It teaches the self-discipline that is needed for a democracy to function. If you can't make decisions about your own life, a skill the military teaches you very well, how can you make decisions that will affect the lives of your fellow citizens? In the event of a major war, we will need millions of trained men and women. In the past, because of the two great oceans that surround us, and the relatively primitive technology of the time, we

136

had several months to gear up for a fight. In the event of a future major conflict, we will only have a matter of weeks, or even days, to get up to speed. Given how sophisticated modern military equipment has become, and the amount of training that is now needed to operate it, a large reserve to back up our armed forces is vital to ensure our national survival and the ideals for which the United States stands.

War has taught me that it is very easy to hate a people merely because they are different. God knows that hatred has started many wars.

I have been a lifelong ham radio enthusiast. For a good deal of my life, I have chatted with people all over the world on just about every imaginable subject. When you are in touch with people from other countries and cultures, it becomes much harder to hate them—a lesson I learned the day I first set foot in Japan. The passion of the human race has always been communication. We have never stopped working on or improving our ability to communicate. The Internet is the latest example of this evolutionary tool. Like a primeval instinct, we have constantly searched for better, more efficient ways to talk to each other. Communication is our future.

As I look back on my half-century in Japan, I'm sad to say that wars fought in the name of racial hatred have not yet ended. The tragedy of Yugoslavia is the best example. Terms such as "final solution," which my generation of Americans fought to eliminate from the lexicon of governments, have been replaced by new ones, like "ethnic cleansing." While the world still contains those people who would murder on a massive scale, the Arsenal of Democracy must remain intact and stand at the ready.

Yet, I am optimistic. In my life, I've seen the world go from being a wild frontier to a city with a few bad neighborhoods. Today, Japanese eat hamburgers and Americans eat sushi. Chinese food is found in most towns, and a growing number of people around the world wear the standard western-style business suit for an important appointment. Slowly but surely, the world seems to be sorting itself out.

Although I've been both the captain of a ship and a captain of industry, I still think of myself as a plain, old sailor with the wind at my back and the stars in the night sky directing me home. But at my age, I think you'd have to call me an ancient mariner. And like the lesson of life taught in that rhyme of old, I've tried to keep my perspective on where I, and everyone else in this world, fit into the grand scheme:

> *He prayeth best who loveth best*
> *all things both great and small.*
> *For the dear God who loveth us*
> *he made and loveth all.*

Notes

1. I was to later learn that it was a failed gambling casino, built during the Depression. Perhaps there were not enough people with money to visit, or perhaps the spirit of the island resented the clumsy intrusion. I like to think it was the latter.

2. I've always wondered if I did the right thing. These days, when addressing an audience of Naval personnel, I ask them the same question. The answers are usually a 50-50 split down the middle.

3. If the gentleman in question is reading this, my belated apologies for any inconvenience caused.

4. "Operation Olympic" was scheduled for the autumn of 1945. "Operation Corona," the invasion of the Kanto region around Tokyo, was to have occurred in the spring of 1946.

5. Tojo had not wanted to shoot himself in the head because, as he would later put it, he had wanted the people to see his face in death.

6. I still have it. It is kept in a safe deposit box in Tokyo. I also carry a photocopy around with me in my wallet.

7. I never did learn its significance. It was never revealed at the trial.

8. Approximately US $2,700 at the time. A hamburger cost ten cents, a bowl of ramen noodle soup cost 20 yen.

9. GIPSEA = G eorge I P urdy — SEA

Index

142

143